# PIMENTO CHEESE:

## *The* **Cookbook**

# PIMENTO CHEESE:
## *The* Cookbook

### 50 RECIPES FROM SNACKS TO MAIN DISHES
### INSPIRED BY THE CLASSIC SOUTHERN FAVORITE

*Perre Coleman Magness*

Photographs by JENNIFER DAVICK

ST. MARTIN'S GRIFFIN
NEW YORK

www.stmartins.com

Book designed by Rita Sowins / Sowins Design

Food photography by Jennifer Davick

Food styling by Marian Cooper Cairns

The Library of Congress Cataloging-in-Publication Data is available
upon request.

ISBN 978-1-250-04729-8 (paper over board)
ISBN 978-1-4668-5734-6 (e-book)

St. Martin's Griffin books may be purchased for educational, business,
or promotional use. For information on bulk purchases, please contact
Macmillan Corporate and Premium Sales Department at 1-800-221-7945,
extension 5442, or write specialmarkets@macmillan.com.

First Edition: September 2014

10 9 8 7 6 5 4 3 2 1

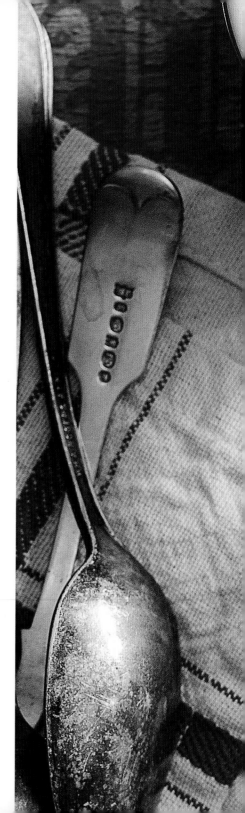

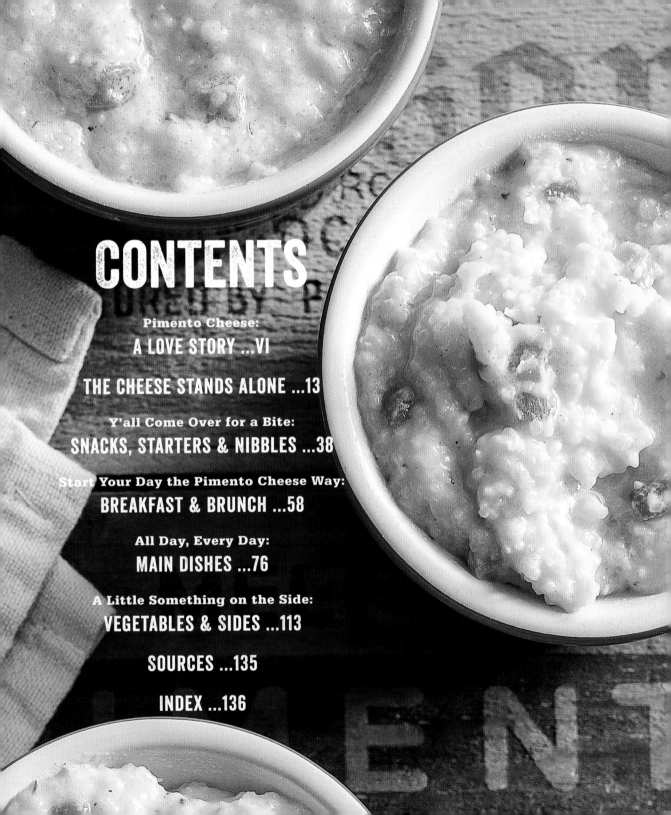

# CONTENTS

# Pimento Cheese:
# A Love Story

**Pimento Cheese is often called the paté of the South. Country classic and city chic.** We Southerners serve it out of a tub with Saltines, or incorporate it into elegant hors d'oeuvres. Meat-and-threes and mom-and-pops sell it between slices of white bread, and upmarket restaurants serve it on platters with house-made charcuterie. It is ubiquitous and useful. It's good to have around when guests are visiting, and an excellent dish to take to a new mother or the recently bereaved.

I am told that pimento cheese is a decidedly Southern delicacy, one of the many and diverse foodways for which the land of my birth is known. I did not know this; not until about fifteen years ago, when I read that fact in a magazine. I, of course, knew about pimento cheese, I just assumed it was universal. You see, I did not grow up in a pimento cheese family. My mother was not a great fan, so it did not feature on our lunch or party menus. As a child, my only encounters with pimento cheese were blobs of red-spotted techno-orange wallpaper glue on white bread at some friend's house. It was the kind of pimento cheese spread purchased in plastic tubs from that top shelf in the dairy aisle, you know, next to the Limburger and neon yellow egg salad. That was my experience of pimento cheese, and I had no real interest in exploring its possible virtues. I also had a childhood adversity to mayonnaise, which in retrospect I cannot fathom. Ah, the years of wasted youth.

As an adult, I discovered that many people around me have strong opinions on pimento cheese: fond childhood memories of Grandma's homemade pimento cheese, or closely held secret ingredients that make their own family recipe unique. I couldn't help but be curious. Had I really missed something? Then the showers started to fall in my life—bridal showers, baby showers—almost nonstop for a large section of my twenties. Pimento cheese figured heavily at these events. It is considered easy to prepare, delicious, and something everyone likes. So I started to try the little finger sandwiches, or delicate molds of pimento cheese served with crackers, sometimes even celery sticks stuffed with the mix, and I had a revelation—it's good. Like stupid good. So I set out to become something of an expert.

Pimento cheese is immutable (cheese, pimentos, mayonnaise) and yet somehow permutable. At the heart of this is the fact that the flavor combination is a good one. Tangy sharp cheese, peppers with bite, but not heat, and creamy mayonnaise just work together—and wonderfully. So taking the flavor combination and applying it to other dishes just seems natural.

## ✳ A Brief History of Pimento Cheese ✳

Like any good Southern tale, pimento cheese has a storied past. It came to us as an exotic ingredient from far-off lands (Spain!), and cheese was expensive, so pimento cheese was the perfect way to outshine our lady friends at dainty teas and formal luncheons. But resourceful Southerners always find a way, and Georgia farmers started growing pimento peppers to bring down the price of our favorite sandwich.

But when the hard times hit, we dug into our deep inner reserves, swearing we would never go hungry again, and turned those simple sandwiches into a profit center during times of war and the Depression. Making sandwiches, craftily wrapped in grease paper, to sell to the workers at North Carolina cloth mills became an acceptable earner for housewives, a business that was still considered ladylike and charming. I imagine the proper pimento cheese purveyor could still wear her pearls to work. That's how Duke's Mayonnaise, the preferred pimento cheese binding agent, came into being—as a big hit on sandwiches sold by a genteel lady to soldiers during World War I.

The first mention of red peppers mixed with cheese in a recipe book appears to be in *Mrs. Hill's Southern Practical Cookery and Receipt Book*, originally published in 1867, which recommends adding pepper as a way to keep cheese fresh before the advent of refrigeration. It wasn't until around 1908, when the business of canning pimentos in the United States began, that recipes using them started to proliferate. Pimentos became a "fancy" ingredient, with their exotic whiff of distant lands. Everyone from Fanny Farmer to Mrs. R. S. Dull mentions them in many recipes. Not many early cookbooks have recipes for pimento cheese spread, and my surmise is that it was something so pedestrian, so automatic in the kitchen, that it did not merit a formal recipe.

My research into the subject leads me to lay out this history of pimento cheese. As with many iconic dishes, pimento cheese started out in home kitchens as cheese mixed with peppers and mayonnaise. But its popularity eventually led it to be commercially produced by the aforementioned female entrepreneurs, who took that homemade staple and turned it into income. These businesses grew and turned into going concerns that sold pimento cheese sandwiches, and then spread to the newly burgeoning supermarket chains. Big producers picked up on it. Cream cheese manufacturers outside the South added pimentos to their product to expand their offerings. When processed-cheese foods hit the scene, pimento was an obvious flavor to incorporate. But in homes across the South, people (mostly women) were still mixing up bowls of their own particular pimento cheese. As time moved on, Depression, war, the convenience-food craze, and the

rise of gourmet foods changed the tastes of the buying public, and the popularity of those prepackaged sandwiches and "salads" like pimento cheese waned, but not at home, and not in the South. So many Southerners have such deeply ingrained memories of pimento cheese, that it was inevitable that chefs from the region who began to explore and celebrate the food of their homeland, rather than excoriate it as old-fashioned and out-of-date, turned to that little orange spread of their childhood. So the everyday staple of so many Southern homes had reached the status of food icon. It is no longer the province of small-town lunch counters, it's now often the most talked-about offering on Manhattan menus.

## ❋ Pimentos ❋

Pimento peppers, or *Capsicum annuum* to be exact, are small, vaguely heart-shaped red peppers. They made up part of the rarefied cargo carried back to Spain from the Americas, and they flourished in that country. I rarely find them here in any other form but jarred, though one grower at my local farmers' market sometimes has a small crop.

The first pimentos in the United States were commercially grown in California beginning in the early 1900s. Soon after, production started up in Georgia, which shortly thereafter eclipsed California in production. Some enterprising farmers set up canning facilities in many parts of the Southeast and pimentos ceased to be a rare delicacy, and became an everyday food commodity. The largest producer of canned and jarred pimentos started, and is still based in my home state of Tennessee. Thomas Moody Dunbar started selling pepper seeds to supplement his small teaching income during the Depression, then moved on to brined peppers and then to pimentos. The company expanded to California and North Carolina and bought up other producers, and now Moody Dunbar, Inc. is the prime pimento purveyor in the country.

For me, pimentos are the essential ingredient to pimento cheese. Without them, well, it's not pimento cheese. I know some chefs and cookbook writers, whom I admire greatly, roast red bell peppers and use them, and some folks substitute chipotles or poblanos and whatnot for the pimentos. While those may be delicious recipes, it just isn't pimento cheese.

### ✳ The Conversion Chart for Pimentos ✳

Throughout the book, I have chosen to list the measurements for pimentos as they are most commonly sold. They are readily found, sliced or diced, in 2-, 4-, and 7-ounce jars. A 4-ounce jar measures just under ½ cup, so if you are measuring from a different container, it is fine to use that amount. A 2-ounce jar is a heaping 2 tablespoons.

### ✳ *I before E . . .* ✳

I have always spelled it this way—P-I-M-E-N-T-O—but I know that many recipes and magazines spell it P-I-M-I-E-N-T-O. I never really paid it much mind, but in the process of writing and researching this book, I thought it might be prudent to suss out the right spelling . . . I couldn't. An online search produced results for both spellings, an informal Facebook poll swayed toward "pimento," but mostly said "who cares, do what you want." I was arguing that I spelled it with no i because that's how it appeared on the jars of pimentos I bought, until I took a second look and realized they do use that extra i. One online sources says *pimiento* is Spanish for "pepper" (pimento is the tree that allspice comes from), while others list both spellings in the same definition. I have a collection of old wooden boxes from different manufacturers that used to hold processed pimento cheese, and they are split on the spelling, too.

In the end, as I could find no definitive reason not to, I stuck with *pimento*, largely because everything I've ever written on the subject uses that spelling, and also to avoid a lot of editing. Besides, in the end, around these parts, no matter the spelling, it's all pronounced "puh-menna" anyway.

## ❋ Paprika: The Pimento's Powdered Cousin ❋

Paprika is made from dried pimento peppers and is most popular in Hungary, where it features in traditional dishes like goulash. Hungarians are the masters of paprika, so many believe the best paprika is Hungarian and it is now widely available. Paprika comes in different varieties: sweet is the most common and what I specify in the majority of recipes. It is mild and deep. Hot paprika is spicy and made with the whole pimento pepper including the seeds. I find half-sharp paprika at Penzey's Spices, which is as it says, somewhere in between, and can be used if you like a little more bite. Smoked paprika, or *pimentón*, is a Spanish specialty made from pimento peppers that are smoked before being ground, and it also comes in mild and hot versions, though I prefer and specify the mild. Pimentón is smoked paprika that comes exclusively from the La Vera region of Spain.

Paprika doesn't have a long shelf life, and frankly, that's why most people probably think of it as only a decorative garnish because the paprika on the spice shelf has been there so long it has no real punch left. Buy small jars and replace them often. In my grandmother's house, it was a venial sin not to garnish a dish with a dash of paprika—sweet paprika, I should specify. This tradition originated in the days before the variety of paprika now on the market was available; no pimentón, no smoked paprika, no ten degrees of Hungarian hot or sweet, just paprika, in the McCormick jar with the green screw top. The folks at McCormick once wisely put out a series of ads in magazines charting the history of their spice packaging so you could figure out how old your spice collection was and throw out those over-two-decades-old bottles. That paprika jar at my grandmother's house didn't even make the chart.

## ❋ Cheese: Where Would We Be Without You? ❋

Cheddar cheese is the most traditional cheese used in pimento cheese. Indeed, some purists might argue that using anything is okay, but that's just plain wrong. I am okay pushing the boat out a little, as long as the anchor is good old cheddar.

Cheddar cheese was born in England, in the town of Cheddar. It dates back to the twelfth century, but became a massed-produced product in the mid-1800s. The production of cheddar-style cheese in America started in the Colonial days and grew with the Westward expansion and opening of cattle-grazing lands.

Originally, the color of cheddar cheese changed seasonally, based on the diet the cows consumed, so each season's production would vary in color. Naturally, cheddar cheese is a yellow color of no particular distinction. Eventually, most cheddar cheese was dyed using annatto seeds to keep that consistent color year-round. Producers of cheddar for large-scale markets upped the dye color to produce the bright orange we know today. Real English Cheddar, however, has a protected status from the European Union and can only be made in certain regions of England and must contain no colorings.

The degrees of cheddar cheese range from mild to extra sharp, and the distinction depends on age. The longer a cheese is aged, the sharper its taste. I specify in recipes which level I prefer. I truly believe that the best classic pimento cheese is made with two kinds of cheddar: the traditional bright orange and the white. I like a combination of extra-sharp, sharp, or medium to give bite.

Always, always grate the cheese to be used for pimento cheese from a fresh block of cheese. Pre-grated bagged cheeses have their place in the world, but this is not it. They are coated with an anticaking agent, which mixes with the mayonnaise and makes the whole affair gummy. A food processor works well for quick grating, a box grater is easier to clean, and pretty fast, too.

## ☀ Mayonnaise: Homemade or Store Bought? ☀

If you want to make good pimento cheese, the mayonnaise must be good. Homemade is wonderful, but let's be honest, that doesn't happen very often. I have discovered that people are fiercely devoted to their particular favorite brand of mayonnaise. I am a devoted fan of Duke's, but was raised on Hellman's, as Duke's was only introduced around here a few years ago.

The key is to look for a brand with as few ingredients as possible, and nothing you can't pronounce. Duke's is particularly good, because there is no added and unnecessary sugar. I make my preference known, but won't engage in the brand battle. Most people tell me they prefer the brand they do because it is what they grew up on, and that's a good enough answer for me. And I also know there are those who will fight me tooth and nail on this, but in my considered opinion, it must be mayonnaise—no sandwich spread, salad dressing, or whip of any kind. Added sugar, corn syrup, and chemicals have no place.

Here is my house-made recipe for mayonnaise, and it could not be simpler (see opposite page).

# HOMEMADE MAYONNAISE

2 LARGE EGG YOLKS

1 TABLESPOON FRESHLY
SQUEEZED LEMON JUICE, OR
WHITE WINE VINEGAR

¼ TEASPOON KOSHER SALT

1 CUP VEGETABLE OIL

*Place the eggs in a food processor and add the lemon juice and salt. Process until combined. With the motor running, gradually add the oil in a thin, steady stream. Process until the mixture is creamy, thick, and emulsified. You will actually hear the food processor change sounds from smooth blending to a wet slapping sound. Scrape the mayonnaise into an airtight container. It will keep in the refrigerator for 3 days.*

**RECIPE NOTES**

» Use a neutral-flavored vegetable oil like canola or grapeseed. Olive oil adds too distinct a flavor, which will compete with the pimento cheese.

» Homemade mayonnaise may not be as thick as store-bought, so add it in increments to your pimento cheese until you achieve your preferred consistency.

» Pimento cheese made with homemade mayonnaise will not stay fresh as long as that made with store-bought mayonnaise, only 3 days. Both, of course, need to be kept refrigerated.

I come from a gadget-loving father, and both my parents are very culinary-minded, so I have been using Cuisinart food processors since my teens. But it was only a few years ago that I discovered this handy tip: The machine has the lid with the feed tube, the big apparatus that fits down in the feed tube called the large pusher, and that has an open tube in the center, and the small pusher that fits in that tube. The small pusher has a little hole in the bottom called the drizzle hole. When making mayonnaise, fit the small pusher into the machine and pour the oil into it. The oil drips out in a perfectly steady stream.

## ✳ To Buy or Not to Buy ✳

This will perhaps be the most controversial section of the book—store-bought pimento cheese. There are many who believe it to be the culinary Antichrist and anathema to all that we hold holy. But there are also many who have the passion and history with pimento cheese who've never had anything but. When I told a Midwestern transplant friend I was working on a pimento cheese cookbook, she was utterly taken aback because she didn't realize it was something people make. She thought it was like M&Ms, a creation of the great industrial machine that could never be duplicated at home.

Since I have taken it as my sacred duty to research all the avenues of pimento cheese available to me, I feel I could not leave this debate out of the discussion. I have bought small-batch, locally made pimento cheese of all varieties, eaten every pimento cheese sandwich on every menu in town, begged it off restaurants that don't normally sell it off menu, and badgered waitresses to find out if it is made in the kitchen or comes on the truck. I have packed it in coolers and carried it home from road trips, and asked friends to do the same. And some of it is quite good. So if you find one you like, made by someone you like, by all means buy it, but you really must learn to make your own, fresh homemade version, too.

And yes, I have purchased massed-produced commercial varieties at the big box stores, mostly to my peril. I have found one that I find acceptable, but the others have frightened me. Those the color of neon hunters' vests do not pass muster. Some were so sweet they brought back unpleasant memories of canned frosting. And upon opening one container, I could clearly see the ridges and whorls from where the smooth goo was spurted from some industrial manufacturing equipment. I couldn't even taste that one.

Many local restaurants and delis make good pimento cheese, and they will sell it by the pound or container. I know of one person who goes well out of her way every week to buy a container of a certain pimento cheese from a certain deli, and she will not be moved to make her own. There is a dedicated pimento cheese vendor at two of our city farmers' markets, in addition to other vendors who offer it as part of their selection. Some of those vendors even sell it at small local groceries.

But I simply must argue that there is no such thing as designer pimento cheese. A fancy cookware catalog has sold a version for $40—that's highway robbery. And a fancy food mail-order catalog has it listed at $22—shipping not included. Neither of these companies, I might add, is based in the South. So this provides yet another reason to make it yourself.

I have timed it with a stopwatch and by the kitchen clock, repeatedly, and making a basic pimento cheese, using store-bought mayonnaise, takes 5 minutes using a food processor and about 8 minutes when grating the cheese by hand. So there really is no excuse. You get exactly what you want in flavor and texture, and you have more control over what goes into it.

# The Cheese Stands Alone

# ✳ Pimento Cheese: Let's Get Personal ✳

Everyone has their favorite recipe for pimento cheese. Maybe their grandmother's recipe, which may have come down from a great-grandmother, or their mother's version, which probably plays heavily on her mother's version. Maybe it has a little less garlic, or a little more mayonnaise. Maybe some newfangled ingredient has been added that would make her mother swoon and give grandmother the vapors. I don't really have a family tradition of pimento cheese. My grandmother, frankly, had help who probably made hers, or she might have bought it from some enterprising lady in her small town. So after I discovered the true beauty and joy of pimento cheese, I set out to make my own version. I took inspiration from all the best versions I'd had. I listened to debates in the kitchen while cleaning up after bridal and baby showers. All cheddar, or both white and yellow? Cream cheese? Onion, or no? Hellman's, Duke's, or homemade mayonnaise? I spoke to caterers, chefs, and cooks. And, woe is me, my lot in life is sometimes unbearable, I sampled pimento cheese everywhere I went.

As I set out on this journey, my aunt (from the non-pimento cheese side of the family, mind you) had a health issue. And, as is always the case, the food from friends and neighbors poured in. I went to visit (and organize the overloaded fridge) and I found no less than five batches of pimento cheese, each completely unique. One was clearly made from the processed cheese that comes in a roll, one had hard-boiled eggs in it, and one had some sort of small crunchy bits—we couldn't decide if they were pumpkin seeds or an accidental bird-food spill. It was a helpful, if painful, learning experience.

So my version, clearly the BEST EVER, combines all the great elements from my studies: Yes to two cheeses, and homemade mayonnaise is best but rare, so use Duke's if you can get it, Hellman's if you can't. I like to grind the pimentos a little, so the flavor is diffused throughout instead of big chunks, and I add nuts for crunch. Lightly seasoned and spiced, it does not require much fiddling around. Now it has become the family pimento cheese. Because it's the best . . . ever. . . really! (See page 17).

# CREAM CHEESE
## PIMENTO CHEESE

4 OUNCES CREAM CHEESE, SOFTENED

8 OUNCES SHARP CHEDDAR, GRATED

¼ CUP MAYONNAISE

ONE 2-OUNCE JAR DICED PIMENTOS, RINSED AND DRAINED

2 TEASPOONS FINELY CHOPPED FRESH PARSLEY

¼ TEASPOON SWEET PAPRIKA

¼ TEASPOON GARLIC POWDER

A FEW GENEROUS GRINDS OF BLACK PEPPER

KOSHER SALT

The earliest form of commercial pimento cheese was pimentos mixed with cream cheese, though eventually that was replaced by processed cheese. I have found many recipes, and spoken to many people who still consider cream cheese an essential ingredient to their favorite pimento cheese, so I include this very simple, thick and creamy version.

*In the bowl of a stand mixer fitted with the paddle attachment, beat the cream cheese on medium speed until smooth. Add the remaining ingredients and mix on medium speed until well combined.*

*The pimento cheese will keep, covered, in the refrigerator for 1 week.*

 *Humble Beginnings*

There are very few combinations on Earth as humble as cheddar, mayonnaise, and pimentos that result in something so fine. Once you taste good pimento cheese, you'll crave it forever.

—REBECCA LANG, author and Southern cooking authority

# PC'S
# PIMENTO CHEESE

1 CUP PECAN HALVES

ONE 2-OUNCE JAR CHOPPED PIMENTOS WITH THEIR LIQUID

2 TEASPOONS GARLIC SALT

DASH OF CAYENNE PEPPER, OR A SHOT OF HOT SAUCE

8 OUNCES EXTRA-SHARP CHEDDAR CHEESE

8 OUNCES SHARP WHITE CHEDDAR CHEESE

1 CUP MAYONNAISE, MORE OR LESS

**RECIPE NOTE**

The most popular and traditional way to serve pimento cheese is in a simple sandwich on plain white bread. For a ladies' lunch or tea party, remove the crusts and slice the sandwich into delicate fingers. A plate of pimento cheese with Saltine crackers feeds bigger crowds at tailgates and buffets. Celery sticks stuffed with pimento cheese is considered by many the "fancy" way to serve it.

My name is Perre Coleman Magness, the fourth in line to carry it forward. That is to say, my great-grandmother, grandmother, and mother were and are all Perre Coleman. Perre Coleman is a double name in real Southern style, so my family, for most of my life, has always called me Perre Coleman. Sometime in later life, my brother started referring to me simply as PC. His friends picked up on it (some didn't know what the initials stood for at first). Our mutual friends picked it up, then my family, then my friends who had no connection to my family. Now I am universally PC. I am Aunt PC to my nieces and nephew and honorary versions, I sign notes and e-mails PC, I leave voice messages from PC. I am listed as PC in almost everyone's contacts. Heck, I even use PC as a monogram. So you can just call me PC, too.

But it was not by design that this PC developed an obsession for the other PC, pimento cheese. I think it is just an amazing piece of Southern serendipity, and some of it starts here, with my personal house blend of pimento cheese, developed in many kitchens over many years. I veer from the doctrinally traditional by simplifying with the food processor, and by adding nuts, which some purists might consider sacrilege.

*Place the pecans and pimentos with their liquid, garlic salt, and cayenne to taste in a food processor fitted with the metal blade and pulse a few times to chop the nuts and blend the pimentos; do not let the mixture turn into a paste.*

*Remove the metal blade and fit the processor with the grating disk. Grate the cheeses. Turn the mixture into a bowl, scraping down the sides of the processor bowl well. Add the mayonnaise, a little at a time, and stir to blend until you reach the desired consistency.*

*The pimento cheese will keep, refrigerated, in an airtight container for 1 week.*

## Ours Is the Best

I have had the good fortune to attend the Southern Food Writing Conference on the complete other side of long, thin Tennessee. I always wrap up my weekend in the mountains with a trip to the Market Square Farmers' Market in Knoxville to stock up on some of my favorite regional foods. At the booth of one of the country's top restaurants, where they sell their amazing cheeses and provisions, I was waiting for the pimento cheese to be unpacked (I had to have some, right?), so I asked the three lovely ladies working the booth about their favorite pimento cheese. They all loyally said "ours is the best," but then I asked them how they made pimento cheese at home. One told me her mother made it with mustard, which is something I had not heard about before. So I asked, "Is that pretty standard around here?" She and her colleague nodded yes. Sure enough, when I got home with my tub of pimento cheese made by the famous restaurant in the other side of the state, mustard was on the ingredient list.

# THREE-CHEESE
## PIMENTO CHEESE

½ CUP MAYONNAISE

ONE 4-OUNCE JAR DICED
PIMENTOS AND THEIR LIQUID

1 GARLIC CLOVE

1 TEASPOON APPLE CIDER
VINEGAR

½ TEASPOON SWEET PAPRIKA

A FEW GENEROUS GRINDINGS
OF BLACK PEPPER

8 OUNCES EXTRA-SHARP
CHEDDAR CHEESE

8 OUNCES GOUDA CHEESE

4 OUNCES GRUYÈRE CHEESE

KOSHER SALT, IF NEEDED

The rich flavor in this blend comes from the combination of cheeses: sharp cheddar, creamy Gouda, and nutty Gruyère. A bit of garlic and a splash of vinegar set off the tangy pimentos, and a hit of paprika adds color and interest.

◇◇◇◇◇◇◇◇◇◇◇◇◇◇◇◇◇◇◇◇◇◇◇◇◇◇◇◇◇◇◇◇◇◇◇◇◇◇◇◇◇◇◇◇◇◇◇◇◇◇◇◇◇◇◇◇

*Mix together the mayonnaise and pimentos with their liquid in a large bowl. Pass the garlic clove through a garlic press, or chop with a sharp knife and work it into a fine paste. Stir the garlic into the mayonnaise and add the vinegar, paprika, and black pepper.*

*Grate the cheeses together in a food processor using the grating disk, or by hand. Toss them together to combine them evenly. Add the cheese to the mayonnaise in the bowl and stir to mix everything together thoroughly. Make sure there are no clumps of cheese that have not been coated with the mayo. Taste and season with some salt if you think it's needed and stir again. Transfer to an airtight container, or tightly cover the bowl, and refrigerate for at least 4 hours to let the flavors meld.*

*The pimento cheese will keep, refrigerated, in an airtight container for 1 week.*

# ROASTED GARLIC
## PIMENTO CHEESE

24 GARLIC CLOVES, PEELED

½ TEASPOON OLIVE OIL

ONE 4-OUNCE JAR DICED
PIMENTOS, RINSED AND
DRAINED

1 CUP MAYONNAISE

½ TEASPOON SWEET PAPRIKA

8 OUNCES SHARP WHITE
CHEDDAR CHEESE

8 OUNCES EXTRA-SHARP
ORANGE CHEDDAR CHEESE

KOSHER SALT

This is a simple version, flavored primarily with sweet and savory roasted garlic. Twenty-four cloves may sound overwhelming, but when roasted, garlic takes on a gentle, rich flavor with none of the sharpness of raw. I happily use pre-peeled garlic cloves bought at the market.

*Preheat the oven to 350°F.*

*Place the garlic cloves on the center of a piece of aluminum foil. Toss them with the olive oil, then pull up the sides of the foil and twist closed to make a little hobo packet. Roast the garlic in the oven for 30 to 40 minutes until it is soft and golden brown. Cool completely.*

*Put the roasted garlic, half of the jar of pimentos, ½ cup of the mayonnaise, and the paprika in the bowl of a food processor fitted with the metal blade. Process until smooth, scraping down the sides of the bowl a couple of times. Make sure that the garlic is completely blended in.*

*Switch to the grating disk and grate the cheeses. Scrape everything into a large bowl, add the remaining half jar of pimentos, and stir together until well combined. Add the remaining ½ cup mayonnaise, a tablespoon at a time, until you reach the consistency you prefer. Season to taste with salt.*

*The pimento cheese will keep, covered, in the refrigerator for up to 5 days.*

# SMOKY BACON
## PIMENTO CHEESE

6 SMOKED BACON SLICES

8 OUNCES NATURALLY SMOKED ORANGE CHEDDAR CHEESE

8 OUNCES NATURALLY SMOKED WHITE CHEDDAR CHEESE

ONE 4-OUNCE JAR DICED PIMENTOS WITH THEIR LIQUID

1 CUP OF MAYONNAISE, MORE OR LESS

2 TEASPOONS SMOKED PAPRIKA (PIMENTÓN)

1 TEASPOON GARLIC POWDER

2 TEASPOONS WORCESTERSHIRE SAUCE

KOSHER SALT

FRESHLY GROUND BLACK PEPPER

Bacon and pimento cheese go brilliantly together, and this deep, smoky version of PC is always a hit. Try it on a burger for a little bite of heaven. Seek out naturally smoked cheese and bacon for the best, smoky flavor.

*Cook the bacon until crispy and transfer to paper towels to drain. Pat off as much grease as possible with paper towels. Finely chop the bacon.*

*Grate the cheeses together into a large bowl. Stir them together with the bacon pieces and pimentos with their liquid. Stir in the mayonnaise until you have a consistency that appeals to you, then add the paprika, garlic powder, and Worcestershire sauce. Season to taste with salt and black pepper.*

*Scrape the pimento cheese into a serving bowl and chill for several hours to let the flavors meld. The pimento cheese will keep, covered, in the refrigerator for up to 5 days.*

# BARBECUE
## PIMENTO CHEESE

1 TABLESPOON SWEET
PAPRIKA

1 TEASPOON KOSHER SALT

½ TEASPOON CELERY SALT

½ TEASPOON FRESHLY
GROUND BLACK PEPPER

¼ TEASPOON ONION POWDER

¼ TEASPOON CHILI POWDER

¼ TEASPOON CRUSHED RED
PEPPER FLAKES

¼ TEASPOON GARLIC POWDER

⅛ TEASPOON CAYENNE
PEPPER

8 OUNCES SHARP ORANGE
CHEDDAR CHEESE

8 OUNCES NATURALLY
SMOKED ORANGE CHEDDAR
CHEESE

4 SCALLIONS, WHITE AND
SOME GREEN PARTS, FINELY
DICED

1 CUP MAYONNAISE

ONE 4-OUNCE JAR DICED
PIMENTOS, RINSED AND
DRAINED

As a born-and-raised-Memphis girl, my blood runs part barbecue sauce, so any exploration of Southern foodways for me is likely to loop back around to barbecue. And with the finest barbecue to be had five minutes away in every direction, I have never seen the point of smoking my own pig. I do have my own house barbecue spice that I use on everything from pork chops to popcorn, and of course, pimento cheese.

◇◇◇◇◇◇◇◇◇◇◇◇◇◇◇◇◇◇◇◇◇◇◇◇◇◇◇◇◇◇◇◇◇◇◇◇◇◇◇◇◇◇◇◇◇◇◇◇◇

*Mix together all the spices in a small bowl until thoroughly blended.*

*Grate the cheeses together into a large bowl and toss together to combine. Add the scallions and toss again; I find my clean, dry hands the best tool for doing this.*

*Mix the mayonnaise with 2 tablespoons of the spice mix in a small bowl and stir until completely incorporated. Stir the mayonnaise into the cheese mixture until everything is well blended and all the cheese is coated. Stir in the pimentos until they are evenly distributed throughout.*

*Chill the pimento cheese, covered, in the fridge for at least 2 hours to let the flavors meld. The pimento cheese will keep, refrigerated, for up to 1 week.*

---

**RECIPE NOTE**

There will be some spice blend left over. Keep it in an airtight container and sprinkle it over hamburgers, steak, or my favorite, popcorn.

Pimento cheese of any kind is good melted on top of a pulled pork shoulder sandwich.

---

BARBECUE
PIMENTO CHEESE

GREEN CHILE
PIMENTO CHEESE

# GREEN CHILE
## PIMENTO CHEESE

¾ CUP MAYONNAISE

2 TABLESPOONS FINELY CHOPPED FRESH CILANTRO

½ TEASPOON GROUND CUMIN

½ TEASPOON SWEET PAPRIKA

¼ TEASPOON GARLIC POWDER

DASH OF CAYENNE PEPPER

8 OUNCES SHARP ORANGE CHEDDAR CHEESE, GRATED

8 OUNCES SHARP WHITE CHEDDAR CHEESE, GRATED

ONE 4-OUNCE JAR DICED PIMENTOS, RINSED AND DRAINED

ONE 4-OUNCE CAN DICED GREEN CHILES, RINSED AND DRAINED

KOSHER SALT

I have been part of amazing New Year's Eve parties for the last few years hosted by the nicest and most creative couple I know. Every year, they come up with a unique theme that carries through to the handmade invitations, decorations, and the food, and I always offer to help out and bring a dish. The theme for one year was the coming "Mayan apocalypse," much joked about at the time. So I made this spicy version of pimento cheese and called it "Pi-Mayan Cheese." It was a big hit with the guests.

Mix together the mayonnaise, cilantro, cumin, paprika, garlic powder, and cayenne in a large bowl until thoroughly combined. Add the cheese, pimentos, and green chiles and stir until everything is evenly distributed. Season to taste with salt.

Cover and refrigerate for several hours to allow the flavors to meld. The pimento cheese will keep covered, in the refrigerator, for 5 days.

> **RECIPE NOTE**
>
> This spicy version of pimento cheese is also great served on top of a hot dog, and so good that it is currently used to top "Perre's Pimento Cheese Dog" at my local taco/hot dog restaurant.

# COMEBACK
## PIMENTO CHEESE

½ CUP MAYONNAISE

2 TABLESPOONS CHILI SAUCE
(SUCH AS HEINZ)

1 TABLESPOON KETCHUP

1 TEASPOON STONE-GROUND
MUSTARD, OR PREPARED
YELLOW MUSTARD

1 TEASPOON
WORCESTERSHIRE SAUCE

1 GARLIC CLOVE, PUT
THROUGH A PRESS OR VERY
FINELY MINCED

DASH OF HOT SAUCE

ONE 2-OUNCE JAR DICED
PIMENTOS, RINSED AND
DRAINED

12 OUNCES SHARP CHEDDAR
CHEESE, GRATED

¼ CUP GRATED ONION
(SEE RECIPE NOTE)

**RECIPE NOTE**

Grate about one-quarter
of a sweet yellow onion
on the same holes of the
grater you use for the
cheese, trying to capture
any juice. Add it all to the
mix and stir well to distribute evenly.

Comeback Sauce is a specialty of Mississippi, and as you meander through the Delta, you find it on some restaurant menus as a sauce or dip with chicken tenders, fried dill pickles, and the like. And, of course, it shows up in community cookbooks in many forms with many uses. The ingredients for Comeback Sauce blend perfectly with sharp cheddar for a truly regional pimento cheese. This is a really punchy version, with sweet chili heat and onion tang.

*Stir together the mayonnaise, chili sauce, ketchup, mustard, Worcestershire sauce, garlic, and hot sauce in a large bowl. Add the pimentos, cheese, and onion and stir to blend thoroughly and evenly.*

*Cover and refrigerate for several hours to allow the flavors to meld. The pimento cheese will keep covered, in the refrigerator for up to 1 week.*

 *Anyplace at Anytime!*

For the past few years my best friend from college (whose family continues to grow with kids) and I meet at the beach, and the first thing we make is pimento cheese to munch on all week. That is what pimento cheese makes me think of!

—ANNA, Memphis, Tennessee

CREOLE
PIMENTO CHEESE

Makes 3½ cups

# CREOLE
## PIMENTO CHEESE

¼ CUP SEEDED AND FINELY
DICED GREEN BELL PEPPER

¼ CUP FINELY DICED WHITE
ONION

¼ CUP FINELY DICED CELERY

ONE 4-OUNCE JAR DICED
PIMENTOS, RINSED AND
DRAINED

1 CUP MAYONNAISE

1½ TEASPOONS CREOLE
SEASONING

DASH OF LOUISIANA HOT
SAUCE

8 OUNCES EXTRA-SHARP
WHITE CHEDDAR CHEESE,
GRATED

8 OUNCES SHARP ORANGE
CHEDDAR CHEESE, GRATED

As is wont to happen when Southerners gather at a table, this time at the Southern Foodways Alliance Symposium, a discussion of pimento cheese arose. Each member of the party was swooning over the importance of pimento cheese and their favorite versions. But one fellow at the table was a little sheepish. Sure, he loves pimento cheese now, but it wasn't something he grew up on. He hailed from southern Louisiana, where he says pimento cheese is not as ubiquitous. But I took this as a challenge, knowing I could incorporate the flavors of Louisiana into a pimento cheese. The "trinity" of celery, green bell pepper, and onion with red pimentos and spicy Creole seasoning makes a jazzy and pretty version with a nice crunch.

*Combine the bell pepper, onion, celery, and pimentos in a large bowl. Stir in the mayonnaise, Creole seasoning, and hot sauce. Add the cheddar cheeses and stir until combined and all the ingredients are well distributed.*

*Cover and refrigerate for a few hours to allow the flavors to meld. The pimento cheese will keep in the refrigerator for five days.*

> **RECIPE NOTE**
>
> You will need about half of a pepper, a quarter of an onion, and 1 stick of celery. As a time-saver, I finely chop the whole of each vegetable, measure what's needed into a bowl. Then I combine the leftovers in a zip-top bag, and freeze it for the next time I want a little "trinity" to start a Louisiana dish.

# PICKLE
## PIMENTO CHEESE

8 OUNCES SHARP ORANGE CHEDDAR CHEESE, GRATED

ONE 2-OUNCE JAR DICED PIMENTOS, RINSED AND DRAINED

1 GARLIC CLOVE, VERY FINELY MINCED

2 TABLESPOONS SWEET PICKLE RELISH (SUCH AS NORTH CAROLINA'S MT. OLIVE BRAND)

1 TABLESPOON JUICE FROM THE PICKLE RELISH JAR

½ CUP MAYONNAISE

This is my least favorite version of pimento cheese only because I don't much like pickles. However, a number of people have told me that the secret to their family pimento cheese recipe is pickles. Some use chopped dill pickles, some just add pickle brine to the mayonnaise, but most use pickle relish, and many of these pickle preparations for pimento cheese appear in Southern community cookbook recipes. So I figured I had to include it. I chose pickle relish, because it figures in many other classic Southern recipes, like deviled eggs and potato salad, so there must be some sort of Southern affinity for it.

*Stir together all the ingredients in a large bowl until thoroughly combined and evenly distributed. Refrigerate for several hours to allow the flavors to blend.*

*The pimento cheese will keep, covered, in the refrigerator for up to 1 week.*

PICKLE
PIMENTO CHEESE

# BUTTERY
## PIMENTO CHEESE

8 TABLESPOONS (1 STICK)
UNSALTED BUTTER, AT ROOM
TEMPERATURE

8 OUNCES EXTRA-SHARP
WHITE CHEDDAR CHEESE,
GRATED

8 OUNCES SHARP ORANGE
CHEDDAR, GRATED

ONE 4-OUNCE JAR DICED
PIMENTOS, RINSED AND
DRAINED

¼ CUP MAYONNAISE

1 TABLESPOON DIJON
MUSTARD

1 TEASPOON WHITE WINE
VINEGAR

¼ TEASPOON KOSHER SALT

DASH OF HOT SAUCE

FRESHLY GROUND BLACK
PEPPER

---

**RECIPE NOTE**

"Rat cheese," mentioned
in a number of old com-
munity cookbooks, refers
to a cheap processed
cheddar cheese. It was so
cheap, it wasn't consid-
ered wasteful to use it in
rattraps.

---

Every Southern community cookbook in my extensive collection has at least
one, if not many, recipes for pimento cheese, and the many ways the three
basic ingredients are configured is fascinating. In one of these, there is a
recipe for "Pimento Cheese Spread" that involves margarine, sandwich
spread, and rat cheese. Since I feel honor bound to explore all permutations
of pimento cheese, I updated that recipe and tinkered a bit with a very good
result. The butter adds richness, of course, but is also a good binder, making
this a particularly good spread for little tea sandwiches. A touch of vinegar and
hot sauce cut the richness.

*Add all the ingredients to the bowl of a stand mixer fitted with the paddle at-
tachment and beat on medium speed until smooth.*

*Transfer to an airtight container. The pimento cheese will keep, covered, in the
refrigerator for up to 5 days.*

 *Grandmother's Pimento Cheese*

My grandmother used to make pimento cheese in a meat grind-
er—you know, one of those things you attach to the counter. The
texture was kind of chunky, not like any other I've had. And listen
to this, she used to serve it to us on cinnamon-raisin bread. I know,
I know, it sounds weird, but it was really good. I mean, that's serious comfort food to me.

—HALL, Memphis, Tennessee

# BUTTERMILK
## PIMENTO CHEESE

1 POUND SHARP ORANGE
CHEDDAR CHEESE, COARSELY
GRATED

1 CUP WHOLE BUTTERMILK,
WELL SHAKEN AND COLD

ONE 4-OUNCE JAR DICED
PIMENTOS, RINSED, DRAINED,
AND PATTED DRY

A FEW GENEROUS GRINDS OF
BLACK PEPPER

Some years ago, eating pimento cheese sandwiches for lunch with friends, a discussion started about pimento cheese, each of us detailing our individual recipes. One friend noted that someone in her family, I can't remember who, made it with buttermilk—no mayo, just buttermilk. I found that a little hard to believe, but filed it away in my memory bank because I love all things buttermilk. This version is extra tangy and creamy and seriously Southern. I guarantee that your friends will be impressed and never guess your secret. I fiddled around with it, adding spices and other ingredients, but found that they competed too much with the beautiful edge of buttermilk, but a big grinding of fresh black pepper fits in just perfectly.

*Beat the cheese and buttermilk together in a stand mixer fitted with the paddle attachment or with an electric hand mixer until fluffy and well combined. Add the drained pimentos and the black pepper and beat, scraping down the bowl as needed, until everything is combined and fluffy. Transfer to an airtight container and refrigerate for a few hours until firm. This is best served cold, right out of the fridge, as it is a bit softer than mayonnaise-based versions.*

# PIMENTO
## BEER CHEESE

1 POUND SHARP ORANGE
CHEDDAR CHEESE

ONE 4-OUNCE JAR DICED
PIMENTOS, RINSED AND
DRAINED

2 GARLIC CLOVES

1 TABLESPOON
WORCESTERSHIRE SAUCE

½ TEASPOON KOSHER SALT

1 TEASPOON SWEET PAPRIKA

DASH OR 2 OF HOT SAUCE

½ CUP BEER, PREFERABLY
LAGER

Pimento cheese in any form is a great tailgate take-along, but add beer and it is perfect game-watching fare. This is great served with pretzels or apple slices, but I also particularly like it spread on a hamburger bun to melt over the meat. The bonus here is that the recipe only uses some of a bottle of beer—you'll probably want to drink the rest.

Cut the cheese into small chunks and put into the bowl of a food processor. Add the pimentos, garlic, Worcestershire sauce, salt, paprika, and hot sauce to taste and process just until it starts to break up and form a paste. Scrape down the sides of the bowl, then start the food processor and drizzle in the beer until the mixture is smooth and creamy. Scrape the beer cheese into a container, cover, and refrigerate for 2 hours, or until the cheese is firm and the flavors have melded.

Serve cold. The beer cheese will keep, covered, in the refrigerator for 1 week.

# LOW-FAT
## PIMENTO CHEESE

3 OUNCES REDUCED-FAT CREAM CHEESE, AT ROOM TEMPERATURE

ONE 6-OUNCE CONTAINER NONFAT PLAIN GREEK-STYLE YOGURT

1 TEASPOON SWEET PAPRIKA

1 TEASPOON ONION POWDER

1 TEASPOON GARLIC POWDER

½ TEASPOON DRY MUSTARD POWDER

½ TEASPOON CELERY SALT

1 TEASPOON WORCESTERSHIRE SAUCE

HOT SAUCE

8 OUNCES REDUCED-FAT SHARP ORANGE CHEDDAR CHEESE, GRATED

8 OUNCES REDUCED-FAT SHARP WHITE CHEDDAR CHEESE, GRATED

ONE 4-OUNCE JAR DICED PIMENTOS, RINSED AND DRAINED

Any nutritionist will tell you that classic pimento cheese is not something you should eat every day. So if you, like me, really like to have a bowl of pimento cheese in your fridge at all times, here's the alternative.

I have attempted lower-fat versions over the years, but never really liked them much, I think because I was using low-fat mayonnaise, which is frankly not very good. But the explosion of Greek-style yogurt onto the grocery scene solved my problem. I only use reduced-fat cheese, because I find fat-free bland and rubbery and not really worth the effort. I go to town with lots of calorie-free spices, so this version packs plenty of punch. You could even add some chopped celery, bell pepper, or onion as in the Creole Pimento Cheese recipe (page 29) to sneak in some vegetables.

*Beat together the cream cheese, yogurt, spices, Worcestershire sauce, and hot sauce to taste in the bowl of a stand mixer fitted with the paddle attachment until smooth and creamy. Scrape down the sides of the bowl, then add the cheeses and pimentos and beat until smooth and combined.*

*Refrigerate for several hours to allow the flavors to meld. The pimento cheese will keep, covered, in the refrigerator for 1 week.*

**RECIPE NOTE**

Leftover cream cheese? Make Cream Cheese Wafer Biscuits: Blend the cream cheese, 1 stick of softened butter, 1 cup of flour, and a pinch of salt in the bowl of a food processor fitted with the metal blade until the dough comes together. Roll the dough up into a log in waxed paper and refrigerate. When chilled, slice and bake until firm and lightly golden. These are an excellent vehicle for pimento cheese.

## → *You Put It Where?*

Pimento cheese has so many uses, it's not just for crackers and sandwiches anymore.

» The Classic. String stalks of celery and cut into pieces about 3 inches long. Fill the cavities with pimento cheese. Serve chilled.

» Rinse and pat dry pickled okra and cut the pods in half lengthwise. Remove any seeds and fill the center of the pods with pimento cheese.

» Carefully pit giant green olives, like Cerignola, and stuff the centers with pimento cheese.

» Hollow out the center of large cherry tomatoes, salt the insides lightly and drain, upside down, on paper towels for about 30 minutes. Fill the tomatoes with pimento cheese.

» Hollow out mushroom caps, fill with pimento cheese, sprinkle bread crumbs over the top. Bake at 350° until the cheese is melty.

» Halve jalapeño peppers lengthwise and scoop out the ribs and seeds. Fill with pimento cheese and wrap with 1½-inch pieces of bacon. Secure with a toothpick and bake at 350° for 20 to 25 minutes.

» Slice thick slices of tomato and set aside to drain on paper towels for about an hour. Spread a generous layer of pimento cheese on top of each tomato slice, transfer to a baking sheet, and run under the broiler until the cheese has browned and is bubbly.

» Spread a thin layer of pimento cheese over store-bought, frozen puff pastry and roll it up into a spiral. Slice the pastry, place the slices on a greased cookie sheet, and bake at 350° until the pastry is done.

» Cut a 4-inch round of pie pastry, place a dollop of pimento cheese on one side, fold over, and crimp the edges. Fry in hot oil (at about 375°) until brown.

» Bake some potatoes at 350° until soft. Cut the potatoes in half lengthwise, then scoop the pulp into a bowl. Mash it well with some pimento cheese, and a drizzle of milk if it needs to be loosened up. Stuff the hollow potato skins with the filling and return the potato to the oven to bake until warmed through.

# Y'all Come Over for a Bite: Snacks, Starters & Nibbles

# SAVORY APPETIZER CHEESECAKE

1 SLEEVE BUTTERY CRACKERS
(LIKE TOWN HOUSE), ABOUT
36 CRACKERS

½ CUP CHOPPED PECANS

8 TABLESPOONS (1 STICK)
UNSALTED BUTTER, MELTED

TWO 8-OUNCE BARS CREAM
CHEESE, SOFTENED

2 LARGE EGGS

1¼ CUPS SOUR CREAM

8 OUNCES SHARP ORANGE
CHEDDAR CHEESE, GRATED

2 GARLIC CLOVES, MINCED

4 SCALLIONS, WHITE AND
LIGHT GREEN PARTS, FINELY
CHOPPED

ONE 4-OUNCE JAR DICED
PIMENTOS, RINSED AND
DRAINED

2 TEASPOONS
WORCESTERSHIRE SAUCE

1 TEASPOON KOSHER SALT

½ TEASPOON SWEET PAPRIKA

A FEW GENEROUS GRINDS OF
BLACK PEPPER

A traditional, if slightly old-fashioned, way of serving pimento cheese more elegantly is to mold it into a ring and serve it on a platter with strawberry jam in the center. This is a more modern and sophisticated version of that classic. You can put strawberry jam on top or on the side, or try a drizzle of Pimento Syrup. See recipe, page 70 (with waffles).

*Preheat the oven to 350°F. Spray a 9-inch springform pan with nonstick spray. Wrap a piece of aluminum foil around the bottom of the pan to catch any dripping butter from the crust.*

*Process the crackers and pecans to fine crumbs in a food processor fitted with the metal blade. Add the melted butter and process until it all comes together. Press the crumbs onto the bottom of the springform pan, pressing the mixture partway up the sides of the pan.*

*Bake the crust for 10 minutes, then transfer to a wire rack to cool.*

*Meanwhile, beat together the cream cheese, eggs, and sour cream in the bowl of a stand mixer fitted with the paddle attachment until smooth. Add the grated cheddar and beat until combined. Add the garlic, scallions, pimentos, Worcestershire sauce, salt, paprika, and black pepper and beat until thoroughly combined.*

*Spread the filling evenly over the crust, and smooth the top. Bake the cheesecake for 30 minutes, or until completely firm. Cool in the pan on a wire rack, then chill in the refrigerator, loosely covered, for several hours or overnight.*

*When ready to serve, release the springform ring and transfer the cheesecake to a platter. Serve with crackers.*

Makes 24 stuffed eggs

# PIMENTO CHEESE STUFFED EGGS

1 DOZEN LARGE EGGS

2 OUNCES EXTRA-SHARP CHEDDAR CHEESE

ONE 2-OUNCE JAR DICED PIMENTOS, RINSED, DRAINED, AND PATTED DRY

1 CUP MAYONNAISE

½ TEASPOON SWEET PAPRIKA, PLUS MORE FOR DECORATION

¼ TEASPOON GARLIC POWDER

KOSHER SALT

FRESHLY GROUND BLACK PEPPER

I don't think a summer picnic would be the same without stuffed eggs; at least not in my family. Recently I served these at a family birthday gathering, and my nephew walked in the house, spotted the eggs, made a beeline past all his family in the room, and immediately stuffed an egg in his mouth. He quickly realized this breech in etiquette and committed another by saying, mouth full, "Hi, Aunt PC, can I have a stuffed egg?"

*Place the eggs in a single layer in a large pot and cover with cold water by 1 inch. Bring to a boil over medium-high heat. When the water comes to a boil, start the timer and cook the eggs for 8 minutes. Meanwhile, fill a large bowl with water and ice. When the 8 minutes are up, using a slotted spoon, transfer the eggs to the ice water and leave the eggs to cool for at least 20 minutes, or up to 30.*

*As the eggs are cooling, grate the cheese on the fine holes of a box grater and let come to room temperature.*

*Roll the cooled eggs on the counter to crack the shells all over. Peel the eggs and rinse under cool water to remove any bits of shell. Pat the eggs dry, then cut in half lengthwise. Gently remove the yolks and transfer to a bowl. Set the whites on a tray waiting to be stuffed.*

*Break the egg yolks up with a fork, add the grated cheese, reserving a little to sprinkle over the tops, then add the mayonnaise. Mash everything together with the fork, then add the paprika, garlic powder, and generous amounts of salt and black pepper to taste. Continue to mash the filling with the fork until smooth. Add the pimentos and stir to distribute them evenly throughout the filling.*

*Fill the egg white halves with the pimento cheese filling, distributing it evenly among the whites. Refrigerate the eggs for at least 1 hour, and up to 4 hours, to firm the filling. You may cover them loosely with plastic wrap. Sprinkle with the reserved cheese and paprika.*

# PIMENTO CHEESE
# CRISPS

ONE 4-OUNCE JAR DICED
PIMENTOS

8 OUNCES SHARP ORANGE
CHEDDAR CHEESE

8 TABLESPOONS (1 STICK)
UNSALTED BUTTER

1½ CUPS ALL-PURPOSE
FLOUR

1 TEASPOON
WORCESTERSHIRE SAUCE

½ TEASPOON GARLIC POWDER

½ TEASPOON SMOKED
PAPRIKA

½ TEASPOON SWEET PAPRIKA

DASH OF CAYENNE PEPPER

A GENEROUS PINCH OF
KOSHER SALT

A FEW GRINDS OF BLACK
PEPPER

½ CUP CHOPPED PECANS

In my ongoing quest to eat as much pimento cheese as possible, I arrive at these little gems. They are a hybrid of two Southern party classics—pimento cheese and the classic cheese straw. Crumbly and cheesy, with the tang of pimentos and the crunch of pecans, they are the perfect nibble with a tall glass of ice tea (or short glass of bourbon). They are wonderful packed up in your heirloom Tupperware for a weekend at the lake, or displayed on your heirloom silver for a shower or a cocktail party. They are a marvelous standby, as you can keep the rolls in the freezer for emergencies, and they make a lovely gift, wrapped up with a ribbon.

*Rinse and drain the pimentos and place them on paper towels. Pat them dry and then leave them for 10 to 15 minutes to air-dry.*

*Grate the cheese and the cold butter together in a food processor fitted with the grating disk. Switch from the grating disk to the metal blade, then add the flour, Worcestershire sauce, garlic powder, smoked and sweet paprikas, cayenne, salt, and black pepper. Process until the dough just begins to come together and looks moist and grainy. Add the pecans and process until the dough begins to pull away from the sides and is about to form a ball. Add the pimentos and pulse a few times just until the dough forms a ball.*

*Dump the dough onto a piece of waxed paper, being sure to scrape out all the pimento pieces. Knead the dough a few times just to incorporate and distribute the pimento pieces. Cut two more lengths of waxed paper, divide the dough into 2 portions and place each portion on one length of waxed paper. Form each dough portion into a log and roll tightly, pressing in the ends to form a nice solid log, and twisting the ends closed like a candy wrapper.*

*Refrigerate the logs for at least 1 hour before baking, but you can refrigerate them for up to 2 days or freeze them for 3 months.*

*(continued)*

*When ready to bake, preheat the oven to 350°F. Line 2 baking sheets with parchment paper.*

*Remove the rolls from the fridge and slice into medium-thick wafers, about ¼ inch each. Place on the baking sheet, allowing a little room between them to spread, and bake until golden around the edges and firm on the top, 10 to 12 minutes. Cool on the pans for a few minutes, then transfer to wire racks to cool completely.*

➤ ## Like Mardi Gras Beads, but Better

Oh, I love pimento cheese. When I was about six or so, this would have been 1947–48, I used to go to the pimento cheese festival in my hometown of Carrollton, Georgia. They had a parade and there was a float, a big flatbed truck, and there were folks on that flatbed making pimento cheese sandwiches and they would toss them to the crowd. Like Mardi Gras beads, but better.

—MILLIE, Atlanta, Georgia

# PIMENTO CHEESE
## DIP

8 OUNCES MEDIUM-SHARP ORANGE CHEDDAR CHEESE

1 CUP SOUR CREAM

1 CUP MAYONNAISE

ONE 4-OUNCE JAR DICED PIMENTOS WITH THEIR LIQUID

2 GARLIC CLOVES

1 TEASPOON WORCESTERSHIRE SAUCE

½ TEASPOON SWEET PAPRIKA

½ TEASPOON KOSHER SALT

POTATO CHIPS, FOR SERVING

CELERY STICKS, FOR SERVING

There is an old drugstore soda fountain here in town where your pimento cheese sandwich comes to you on a paper plate with a bag of off-brand crinkle potato chips. The pimento cheese is good, and the soft white sandwich bread is stuffed full, so some of the filling inevitably falls out onto the plate. After I finish the sandwich, I like to scoop that extra pimento cheese up with those salty chips. This dip is my way of sharing that guilty pleasure.

*Grate the cheese in a food processor fitted with the grating disk. Switch to the metal blade, and add the sour cream, mayonnaise, and pimentos. Pass the garlic through a garlic press or finely mince it with a sharp knife and add to the cheeses. Add the Worcestershire sauce, paprika, and salt. Process the dip until it is almost completely smooth, scraping down the sides of the bowl.*

*Scrape the dip into a bowl. Cover and refrigerate for at least an hour to let the flavors meld. The dip can be made up to a day ahead and stored, covered, in the refrigerator.*

*Serve with potato chips and celery sticks.*

 *The Southern Calling Card*

Here in Boston, I became friends with another woman from my small Tennessee hometown and, for the first several years of our friendship, we brought each other pimento cheese each time we visited each other's homes. It's like a little Southern calling card for expats in New England.

—LONSDALE, Boston, Massachusetts via Columbia, Tennessee

# VIDALIA–PIMENTO CHEESE
# HOT DIP

2 MEDIUM VIDALIA ONIONS,
(ABOUT 1½ POUNDS) DICED

24 OUNCES CREAM CHEESE,
AT ROOM TEMPERATURE

½ CUP MAYONNAISE

8 OUNCES SHARP ORANGE
CHEDDAR CHEESE, GRATED

ONE 7-OUNCE JAR DICED
PIMENTOS, RINSED AND
DRAINED

CORN CHIPS OR TOASTS,
FOR SERVING

I don't know if I have ever been to a party locally that didn't include the original version of this dip. It appears in the ubiquitous Junior League of Memphis cookbook *Heart and Soul* as Hot Onion Soufflé, and it is easy to make, quick, and will be devoured by anyone who comes face-to-face with it. The original recipe calls for Swiss cheese and frozen onions, but I prefer to use the South's own sweet Vidalia onions. This makes a lot of dip, but I have never seen a dish of it that wasn't scraped clean by the end of a party. Big Fritos seem to be the favorite dipper, but it can be served more elegantly with little toasts to spread it on.

Peel the onions and dice them finely. I like a very small ⅛-inch dice so it's easy to pick up the dip with chips. You should have about 4 cups sliced onion.

Beat the cream cheese and mayonnaise together in the bowl of a stand mixer fitted with the paddle attachment until smooth. Add the onions, grated cheddar, and pimentos and beat until everything is well combined, scraping down the sides of the bowl a couple of times during mixing. Scrape the dip into a 9 x 13-inch baking dish.

At this point, you can cover the dip and refrigerate it for up to a day.

When ready to bake, preheat the oven to 350°F. Bake the dip, uncovered, for about 15 minutes, or until heated through and bubbling. Serve with corn chips or little toasts.

## The Southern Ploughman's Platter

Ploughman's Lunch is a classic English pub dish, geared to the hungry working man needing a quick and filling meal. It generally consists of a hunk of crumbly Cheddar cheese, pickle (particularly Branston pickle, if memory serves), or pickled onion and chutney. Maybe there will be a wedge of country bread, possibly a pickled egg, and frequently a slice of ham or rough country pâté, maybe even half a slice of meat pie. Pub food can sometimes be dodgy, but it is hard to ruin a simple ploughman's. So it was a cheap, filling, and frequently delicious treat when I was a student at Oxford.

I visited Charleston a few years ago, and ate at the wonderful Hominy Grill, which serves simple twists to low-country classics in a casual setting. We started the night with an intriguing appetizer selection. I can't remember what it was called; it might have been a picnic plate. But when it came to the table, I immediately thought of it as a Southern Ploughman's. A rough-hewn board with a little jar of pimento cheese, pickled okra, paper-thin slices of salty country ham, multicolored pickled eggs, and flat cornbread cracker crisps. Ingenious and perfect, I tucked that idea away, and it has been a staple at parties at home ever since. I vary it up, sometimes keeping it simple, sometimes going a bit overboard. I scoop my favorite pimento cheese of the moment into an old Mason jar or wire bail jar, and track down some thin pieces of country ham. I pickle eggs simply, not in colorful beet juice or turmeric, and quarter them to add to the display. I open whatever jar of summer pickles I have in the pantry—okra, field peas, corn relish, red pepper jam, chowchow. I make superthin cornbread squares, or maybe miniature biscuits. I have been known to add candied bacon or country ham pâté. The possibilities are endless.

This charmingly elevates simple pimento cheese by pairing it with its natural culinary cousins, and brings a long tradition into the modern age. So think up your own version of the Southern Ploughman's. Just start with good pimento cheese and go from there.

Makes 20 to 24 puffs

# PIMENTO CHEESE
# GOUGÈRES

8 TABLESPOONS (1 STICK)
UNSALTED BUTTER

1 CUP WATER

1 CUP ALL-PURPOSE FLOUR

½ TEASPOON SWEET PAPRIKA

¾ TEASPOON KOSHER SALT

4 LARGE EGGS, AT ROOM
TEMPERATURE

4 OUNCES AGED EXTRA-SHARP
CHEDDAR CHEESE, FINELY
GRATED

ONE 2-OUNCE JAR DICED
PIMENTOS, RINSED, DRAINED,
AND PATTED DRY

COARSE SALT, SUCH AS
MALDON SEA SALT

**RECIPE NOTE**

You can also freeze the
dough for later use. Scoop
the mounds of dough onto
a parchment paper–lined
baking pan and freeze
until firm. Transfer to a
ziplock bag and freeze up
to a month. Bake the puffs
from frozen, adding a few
minutes to the final baking
time.

I had a recipe for gougères when I was a teenager, and I made them all the
time. I thought they were so sophisticated and French and made me look like
a real gourmet. But the recipe eventually fell by the wayside, replaced by
something else I'm sure. Many years later, on a family barge trip in France, we
were welcomed on the boat with champagne and perfect, warm gougères. That
returned them to my repertoire, though I never have found my original teenage
recipe. It seemed only right to "Southernize" these gougères pimento cheese style.

Preheat the oven to 425°F. Line a rimmed baking sheet with parchment paper.

Cut the butter into chunks and put it and the water into a large, sturdy
saucepan. Bring to a boil over high heat, stirring occasionally to melt the
butter. When the butter has melted and the liquid is boiling, reduce the heat to
medium and dump in the flour, paprika, and salt all in one go. Stir vigorously
with a sturdy wooden spoon; it will all come together in a big ball. Continue
cooking for about 2 minutes, stirring constantly. You want to cook out any
raw flour taste. Remove the pan from the heat and let the mixture cool for
about 4 minutes so the eggs won't cook when they come into contact with the
hot dough.

Stir in the eggs, one at a time, until you have a smooth dough a little looser
than what you started with, making sure the eggs are completely incorporated.
Stir in the cheese and the pimentos and mix until everything is completely combined and the pimentos are evenly distributed. This takes a little elbow grease.

Scoop mounds of the dough onto the prepared baking sheets using a cookie
scoop or rounded tablespoon, spacing them about ½ inch apart. Sprinkle the
top of each gougère with a bit of paprika and a pinch of coarse salt. Bake for
10 minutes, then lower the oven temperature to 350°F and bake for 15 minutes more, or until they are puffed and golden and lovely.

Serve warm.

Makes 32 pigs in blankets; ¾ cup dip

# PIGS IN PIMENTO CHEESE BLANKETS
## WITH HONEY-MUSTARD DIP

**HONEY-MUSTARD DIP**

½ CUP MAYONNAISE

¼ CUP PREPARED YELLOW
MUSTARD

2 TABLESPOONS HONEY

**PIGS AND BLANKETS**

ONE 14-OUNCE PACKAGE
COCKTAIL SAUSAGES (SUCH
AS "LIT'L SMOKIES")

ONE 2-OUNCE JAR DICED
PIMENTOS

8 OUNCES SHARP ORANGE
CHEDDAR CHEESE

8 TABLESPOONS (1 STICK)
UNSALTED BUTTER

1 CUP ALL-PURPOSE FLOUR

1 TEASPOON
WORCESTERSHIRE SAUCE

½ TEASPOON SWEET PAPRIKA

½ TEASPOON KOSHER SALT

½ TEASPOON FRESHLY
GROUND BLACK PEPPER

DASH OF CAYENNE PEPPER

Slightly silly, but no less tasty for it, I have served these to kids to rave reviews, but also to grown-ups in a cocktail setting. That garnered giggles, but every last one of the little pigs was gobbled up.

*FIRST MAKE THE DIP: Whisk the ingredients together in a small bowl and refrigerate for several hours to allow the flavors to blend.*

*PREPARE THE PIGS IN BLANKETS: Drain the sausages and pat them dry on paper towels. Set aside to air-dry for about 30 minutes. Rinse and drain the pimentos and pat dry on paper towels as well.*

*Grate the cheese and the butter in a food processor fitted with the grating disk. Switch to the metal blade, and add the flour, Worcestershire sauce, paprika, salt, black pepper, and cayenne. Process until the mixture is crumbly and begins to come together. Add the pimentos and continue processing until the dough forms a ball that pulls away from the sides of the bowl.*

*Pinch about 3 teaspoons of dough off the ball and flatten it into a disk between your palms. Place a sausage in the center of the dough disk and bring it up to cover the sausage. Pinch together to enclose, then roll between your palms to completely seal in the pig. Place the package on a parchment paper–lined rimmed baking sheet and continue with the rest of the dough and sausages. I consistently make about 32 of these from this recipe, which leaves 4 or 5 extra sausages. Consider these the cook's bonus.*

*When all the pigs are in their blankets, transfer the baking sheet to the refrigerator for at least an hour. This will firm the dough and prevent it from spreading during baking. When ready to bake, preheat the oven to 400°F. Bake the pigs for 20 to 25 minutes until the cheese dough is puffy and nicely browned. Serve warm with the Honey-Mustard Dip.*

# BACON–PIMENTO CHEESE
# TRUFFLES

10 BACON SLICES

1 CUP PECAN HALVES

2 TABLESPOONS FRESH
PARSLEY LEAVES

8 OUNCES EXTRA-SHARP
ORANGE CHEDDAR CHEESE

8 OUNCES CREAM CHEESE,
CUT INTO CUBES, AT ROOM
TEMPERATURE

1 TABLESPOON BACON FAT

2 TABLESPOONS SNIPPED
FRESH CHIVES

1 TEASPOON KOSHER SALT

½ TEASPOON SWEET PAPRIKA

¼ TEASPOON CAYENNE
PEPPER

ONE 4-OUNCE JAR DICED
PIMENTOS, RINSED AND
DRAINED

I've been making a pimento cheese ball rolled in bacon and pecans for years. It is an easy standby, take-to-a-party dish. Then I was invited to a party that called for something slightly more interesting than a standard cheese ball, so I fancied it up a bit, making little bite-size truffles served on fancy cocktail picks.

◇◇◇◇◇◇◇◇◇◇◇◇◇◇◇◇◇◇◇◇◇◇◇◇◇◇◇◇◇◇◇◇◇◇◇◇◇◇◇◇◇◇◇◇◇◇◇◇◇◇◇◇◇◇◇

*Preheat the oven to 400°F. Place a wire rack inside a rimmed baking sheet and arrange the bacon slices on the rack. Cook the bacon in the oven until very crispy, 20 to 25 minutes. Transfer the bacon to paper towels to drain, and pat the bacon strips on both sides with paper towels to blot excess fat. Set aside to cool.*

*Break 5 of the bacon slices into pieces and put into the bowl of a food processor fitted with the metal blade. Add ½ cup of the pecan halves and the parsley. Process until the bacon and pecans are the texture of coarse bread crumbs. Scoop the crumbs out onto a flat plate.*

*Switch to the grating disk and grate the cheddar cheese. Switch back to the metal blade, add the cream cheese, the remaining 5 bacon slices, broken into pieces, the remaining ½ cup pecans, the bacon fat, chives, salt, paprika, and cayenne and process until the cheeses begin to come together. Add the pimentos and process until smooth and all the ingredients are incorporated, scraping down the sides of the bowl as necessary.*

*To make the truffles, using your clean hands, shape the cheese mixture into small balls about the size of a quarter, then roll the cheese balls in the bacon crumbs, pressing them into the sides of the balls. Place on a baking sheet and refrigerate until firm. The cheese truffles can be made up to 3 days ahead.*

*Serve with cocktail picks, or in the center of round crackers on an elegant serving platter.*

## Pimento Cheese Butter Balls

I cheat. Sure, I love a quick fix sometimes. And here's a pimento cheesy favorite. I keep a big airtight container of homemade baking mix in my pantry (there are lots of recipes online) so I don't add extra chemicals to my recipes, and use the best small-batch, locally made PC I can find if I don't have any house-made on hand.

Preheat the oven to 350°F. Using a fork, mix together 1 cup baking mix, ¼ cup prepared pimento cheese, and 3 to 4 tablespoons milk until you have a stiff dough. Melt 2 tablespoons of butter in small bowl in a microwave. Roll the dough into 6 balls about the size of golf balls, then roll them in the butter. Place them on a rimmed baking sheet, sprinkle with a little coarse salt, and bake at 350° until firm and golden, about 10 minutes. I like to pull them out of the oven a bit before they are ready, so they are soft and cheesy in the center. I have also baked them in a toaster oven to make it really easy.

# PIMENTO CHEESE
# BAGUETTE BITES

2 TABLESPOONS SLICED
PIMENTOS

3 OUNCES CREAM CHEESE, AT
ROOM TEMPERATURE

¼ CUP MAYONNAISE

2 HEAPING TABLESPOONS
EXTRA-SHARP CHEDDAR
CHEESE, GRATED ON THE FINE
HOLES OF A BOX GRATER

DASH OF SALT

20 TO 25 BAGUETTE ROUNDS,
ABOUT ¼ INCH THICK

PAPRIKA FOR SPRINKLING

Such a simple recipe produces a surprisingly sophisticated result. The topping develops a crackling crust with a creamy layer covering the crispy bread. I would happily pass these around with glasses of champagne.

*Preheat the oven to 350°F.*

*Rinse and drain the pimentos well. Place the pimentos on a double layer of paper towels and pat them as dry as you can get them. Scrape them onto a cutting board and use a sharp knife to chop them as fine as you can. When they are chopped, pat dry with a paper towel again.*

*Beat the cream cheese and mayonnaise together until smooth. Add the cheddar cheese and pimentos and stir to combine. Add a pinch of salt to taste. Sprinkle with paprika. You can make the topping a few hours ahead. Bring to room temperature before spreading.*

*Spread about 1 teaspoon of the mix on each of the bread rounds and place on a baking sheet. Bake for 10 minutes until the topping is lightly browned. Serve immediately.*

# PIMENTO CHEESE
# POPCORN

3 OUNCES SHARP CHEDDAR
CHEESE

1 TEASPOON SWEET PAPRIKA

2 TEASPOONS KOSHER SALT,
PLUS MORE AS NEEDED

8 TO 10 CUPS POPPED
POPCORN, FROM ABOUT
½ CUP KERNELS

4 TABLESPOONS (½ STICK)
UNSALTED BUTTER, MELTED

Piping hot popcorn, whisper-thin shreds of cheese, and perky paprika and you've got great handfuls of pimento cheese flavor.

*Grate the cheese with the finest grater you have. I use a rasp grater that I mainly use for citrus zest, but your box grater may have a very fine side as well; you want whisper-thin strands of cheese. Mix the cheese with the paprika and salt, tossing it around with your clean, dry hands to coat the cheese in the spice and salt. Try to break up any large clumps of cheese as you toss.*

*Pop your corn by your preferred method—stovetop, air popper, or microwave air popper (not microwave bags). It is important that the popcorn be piping hot when you add the seasoning. When the corn is popped, immediately transfer it to a large paper grocery bag. Add the butter (still warm is best) and the seasoned cheese. Fold the top over and shake like crazy to distribute the flavorings. Taste and add a little more salt if you want to.*

*Serve immediately, with lots of paper napkins—that paprika can make your fingers orange!*

# Start Your Day the Pimento Cheese Way:

# Breakfast & Brunch

# PIMENTO CHEESE
# SAUSAGE BALLS

3 CUPS ALL-PURPOSE FLOUR

1½ TABLESPOONS BAKING
POWDER

1 TEASPOON KOSHER SALT

¼ CUP MAYONNAISE

4 TABLESPOONS
(½ STICK) UNSALTED
BUTTER, SOFTENED

1 TABLESPOON DIJON
MUSTARD

1 POUND BULK SAUSAGE

8 OUNCES MEDIUM, ORANGE
CHEDDAR CHEESE, GRATED

ONE 4-OUNCE JAR DICED
PIMENTOS, RINSED AND
DRAINED

Sausage balls are one of my favorite childhood treats. My mom used to make them from a baking mix, sausage, and cheese and keep them in the freezer. She would pop a few in the oven for breakfast or an afternoon snack. As an adult, I often asked her to make these for me as a Christmas gift so I could do the same. I've "pimento-cheesified" the classic, and replaced the baking mix with my own mix with purer ingredients. These are perfect for breakfast or a snack, but also make a great appetizer.

*Preheat oven to 350°F. Line a rimmed baking sheet with parchment paper or nonstick aluminum foil.*

*Put the flour, baking powder, and salt in a large mixing bowl and blend together with a fork. Add the mayonnaise, butter, mustard, sausage, cheese, and pimentos. Using your clean hands, knead the mixture until it comes together. This will take a little elbow grease, but keep at it until all the flour has been kneaded in. The mixture may seem dry, but fat will render out of the sausage while baking, so don't be alarmed.*

*Roll the dough into golf ball–sized balls and place on the lined baking sheet. Bake for 15 to 20 minutes until the balls are golden brown and cooked through.*

*The uncooked balls can also be made ahead, placed on a waxed paper–lined tray, and frozen until hard. Transfer to a zip-top bag and keep in the freezer for up to 3 months. Bake from frozen, increasing the baking time by about 10 minutes.*

# PIMENTO CHEESE
# BISCUITS

2 CUPS ALL-PURPOSE FLOUR, PLUS A BIT FOR SPRINKLING

1 TABLESPOON BAKING POWDER

1 TEASPOON KOSHER SALT

½ TEASPOON SWEET PAPRIKA

½ TEASPOON GARLIC POWDER

12 TABLESPOONS (1½ STICKS) UNSALTED BUTTER, COLD

½ CUP BUTTERMILK, WELL-SHAKEN AND COLD, PLUS A LITTLE FOR BRUSHING

1 LARGE EGG

1 TEASPOON WORCESTERSHIRE SAUCE

1 CUP GRATED EXTRA-SHARP ORANGE CHEDDAR CHEESE

ONE 4-OUNCE JAR DICED PIMENTOS, RINSED, DRAINED AND PATTED DRY

SEA SALT FOR SPRINKLING, PREFERABLY MALDON SEA SALT

The combination of two Southern favorites—the buttermilk biscuit and pimento cheese—is ingenious. Standing in front of the open fridge door the night of a holiday brunch party years ago, I spread some pimento cheese on a leftover biscuit, and it hit me that I could save that pesky spreading step and create a one-bite wonder. These gems are the perfect pairing for a bowl of soup, but it doesn't end there. Try a dab of butter and a little country ham, or a dab of butter and some crispy bacon. Make that candied bacon and you are on your way to heaven. I also make these in little cocktail-size bites and serve them at parties, either with butter alone, or something yummy tucked inside.

◇◇◇◇◇◇◇◇◇◇◇◇◇◇◇◇◇◇◇◇◇◇◇◇◇◇◇◇◇◇◇◇◇◇◇◇◇◇◇◇◇◇◇◇◇◇◇◇◇◇◇◇

*Preheat the oven to 425°F. Line a baking sheet with parchment paper.*

*Put the flour, baking powder, salt, paprika, and garlic powder in the bowl of a stand mixer and stir together with a fork. Cut the butter into small cubes and drop them in the flour. Attach the bowl to the mixer, fitted with the paddle attachment, and blend the butter and flour on low speed until the butter is the size of small BBs. You want some butter blended in, but the visible small pieces of butter will make the biscuits fluffy.*

*Measure the buttermilk in a measuring cup, crack in the egg, add the Worcestershire sauce, and beat it with a fork until the mixture is well blended. With the mixer on low speed, add the buttermilk mixture all at once and blend just until everything is moistened.*

*Toss the cheese with a little flour, and do the same to the pimentos. This step keeps the cheese and pimentos from clumping together so they blend throughout the dough. Drop them both in the mixer and, still on low speed, beat until everything just starts to come together.*

*(continued)*

*Dump the dough onto a well-floured surface and gently bring it all together, kneading just a few times. Handle it with care and don't overwork the dough, or the biscuits will be tough. A few pimentos may stick to the board or fall out; just stick 'em back in. Pat the dough into a rectangle about 6 x 10 inches, using the back of a large knife or bench scraper to square off the ends. Flour the knife or scraper, and cut the dough into 8 squares (see Recipe Note). Place the biscuits on the prepared baking sheet, lightly brush the tops with a little buttermilk, and sprinkle with sea salt.*

*Bake the biscuits for 15 to 20 minutes until lightly browned and baked through. Serve warm, or wrap tightly and store in an airtight container. Reheat gently before serving.*

**RECIPE NOTE**

I generally cut these into squares to avoid wasting or rerolling dough, but if you prefer, you can cut them into rounds as you would a regular biscuit.

# PIMENTO CHEESE
## BREAD

1 CUP BUTTERMILK

1 CUP WATER

2 TABLESPOONS UNSALTED BUTTER

4½ TO 5½ CUPS ALL-PURPOSE FLOUR

3 TABLESPOONS SUGAR

1½ TABLESPOONS ACTIVE DRY YEAST

1 TABLESPOON KOSHER SALT

½ TEASPOON SWEET PAPRIKA

1½ CUPS GRATED EXTRA-SHARP CHEDDAR CHEESE

1 LARGE EGG

ONE 4-OUNCE JAR DICED PIMENTOS, RINSED AND DRAINED

I love hot, fresh bread—the smell while it is baking, the butter melting into the crannies of a warm slice—but I am by no means a master baker, and have yet to fully uncover the mysteries of yeast. So simple, no-knead breads are my kitchen staple, and using the mixer to cut down on the beating is the way to go.

Combine the buttermilk, water, and butter in a small saucepan and heat over low heat. Cook, stirring frequently, just until the butter has melted and the liquid is barely simmering (about 110°F).

Meanwhile, put 2 cups of flour, the sugar, yeast, and salt into the bowl of a stand mixer fitted with the paddle attachment and stir to combine. When the buttermilk mixture is heated, pour it into the mixer bowl and beat on medium speed for 2 minutes, scraping down the sides of the bowl a couple of times.

Turn the mixer off and add the paprika, cheese, ½ cup of the flour, the egg, and the pimentos. Increase the mixer to high and beat another 2 minutes, scraping down the sides of the bowl halfway through.

With the mixer on its lowest setting, add enough flour, ½ cup at a time, to make a sticky, shaggy dough that clings to the paddle. Stop and pull the dough off the paddle a couple of times and keep stirring.

Transfer the dough to a clean, buttered bowl and cover it tightly with plastic wrap. Leave it in a warm place to rise until doubled in volume, about 1 hour (see Recipe Note).

Preheat the oven to 350°F. Line a baking sheet with parchment paper.

(continued)

*Punch down the risen dough, turning it over on itself a couple of times. Form
it into a round or a long loaf shape and transfer it to the lined baking sheet.
Bake for 60 to 70 minutes until it is brown and firm. When you tap on the bottom of the loaf, it should give a nice hollow thud.*

 *Leftover Bread?*

Leftover bread? Make Pimento Cheese Pain Perdu by soaking a
few slices of this bread in eggs beaten with milk, then pan-fry
them until crispy in a little butter. Serve with Pimento Syrup
(see page 70).

This bread also makes an amazing BLT.

# PIMENTO CHEESE
# SAUSAGE CASSEROLE

1 POUND BULK SAUSAGE MEAT

1½ CUPS DICED YELLOW ONION (ABOUT 1 MEDIUM ONION)

¼ CUP WATER

12 SLICES WHITE SANDWICH BREAD

ONE 4-OUNCE JAR DICED PIMENTOS, RINSED AND DRAINED

8 OUNCES SHARP ORANGE CHEDDAR CHEESE, GRATED

¼ CUP CHOPPED FRESH PARSLEY

5 LARGE EGGS

2⅓ CUPS WHOLE MILK

1 TABLESPOON MAYONNAISE

1 TABLESPOON DIJON MUSTARD

1 TEASPOON WORCESTERSHIRE SAUCE

½ TEASPOON SWEET PAPRIKA

½ TEASPOON DRY MUSTARD POWDER

½ TEASPOON KOSHER SALT

½ TEASPOON FRESHLY GROUND BLACK PEPPER

I can't remember a Christmas morning that didn't feature some version of this casserole. It is simple to make and can be done ahead of time. It is hearty, filling, and comforting, and speaks to me of family, happiness, and celebration.

*Crumble the sausage meat into a spacious skillet and cook until browned and no longer pink on the inside. Continue to break up the sausage meat into bite-size pieces as you cook. Using a slotted spoon, transfer the cooked sausage to a paper towel–lined plate. Discard all but 1 tablespoon of the fat from the skillet. Leave the fat in the skillet off the heat for a few minutes, then add the onions and return to medium-high heat. Cook until the onions are soft and beginning to brown ever so slightly. Add the water and stir well. Cook until the water has evaporated and the onions are a light toffee color and very soft. Set aside to cool.*

*Remove the crusts from the bread and cut the slices into small pieces; I'd say 3 cuts across and 3 cuts down. Sprinkle the bread cubes into a greased 9 x 13-inch baking dish. When the onions have cooled, stir in the cooked sausage and pimentos and mix until evenly distributed. Add the sausage mixture, cheese, and parsley to the bread in the dish and use your hands to toss everything around until all the ingredients are evenly distributed.*

*Whisk the eggs in a medium bowl, then add the milk and remaining ingredients and then whisk again until everything is thoroughly combined. If there are some small lumps of mayo, that's fine. Pour the eggy mix evenly over the mixture in the baking dish, then lightly press down on the bread to submerge it in the liquid. Cover the baking dish with aluminum foil and refrigerate 8 hours or overnight.*

*When ready to bake the casserole, remove the baking dish from the fridge while you preheat the oven to 350°F. Bake the casserole, covered, for 20 minutes, then remove the foil and bake for 30 to 40 minutes more until it is set and golden.*

# EGGS BENEDICT
## WITH PIMENTO HOLLANDAISE AND CHEDDAR

### PIMENTO HOLLANDAISE

ONE 4-OUNCE JAR DICED
PIMENTOS

2 LARGE EGG YOLKS

16 TABLESPOONS (2 STICKS)
UNSALTED BUTTER

1 TEASPOON FRESHLY
SQUEEZED LEMON JUICE

KOSHER SALT

### EGGS

4 LARGE WHOLE EGGS, AT
ROOM TEMPERATURE

2 TABLESPOONS WHITE
VINEGAR

### ASSEMBLY

2 ENGLISH MUFFINS

2 TEASPOONS MAYONNAISE

SWEET PAPRIKA

4 OUNCES SHARP CHEDDAR
CHEESE, FINELY GRATED,
PLUS MORE FOR SPRINKLING

8 COOKED BACON SLICES, OR
4 SLICES CANADIAN BACON
OR COUNTRY HAM BISCUIT
SLICES

Pimento cheese can be rendered as a fancy dish, too. At least, I always think of Eggs Benedict as a fancy dish, because I mostly have it on the rare occasions I go to a restaurant for brunch. And I always have some form of it when I visit New Orleans. But it occurred to me that I could build a better "benny" PC style, and in the process I discovered making your own Eggs Benedict isn't really all that difficult.

MAKE THE HOLLANDAISE: Rinse and drain the pimentos, pat dry on paper towels and set aside to air-dry. When the pimentos are dry, put them in the jar of a blender with the egg yolks. In a small saucepan, melt the butter over medium heat until it is bubbling; do not boil or allow to brown. Remove the center plug from the lid of the blender, return the lid to the blender. Turn the motor on, and very slowly drizzle in the melted butter in a steady stream. When all the butter is incorporated and the sauce is thick and emulsified, add the lemon juice and a generous pinch of salt and blend in. To keep the sauce warm for up to 30 minutes, pour it into a measuring cup and place the measuring cup in a larger bowl of warm water. Do not let any water get into the sauce.

POACH THE EGGS: Fill a large, wide skillet with a tight-fitting lid with about 4 inches of water and add 2 teaspoons of white vinegar. Bring the water to a simmer, not a boil; just bubbling, shivering heat. Crack each egg into a small dish and carefully slide the egg into the water. Cover the pan and remove it from the heat. Leave the eggs, undisturbed, for 5 minutes, then lift the lid and check that the whites are set. Cover again for a few more minutes if needed. Lift the eggs out of the pan with a slotted spoon and pat the bottoms dry on a clean towel.

(continued)

*TO ASSEMBLE: Split the English muffins in half and spread each half with a ½ teaspoon of the mayonnaise; you just want a thin slick of mayo. Sprinkle each with a little paprika. Spread 1 ounce of grated cheese on top of each muffin half. Place the muffin halves on a baking sheet and toast until the cheese is melted. Divide the bacon, ham, or Canadian bacon equally among each half, then top with the poached eggs. Spoon over the warm hollandaise, sprinkle the tops with a little extra grated cheese and a dash of paprika and serve immediately.*

**RECIPE NOTE**

This Pimento Hollandaise is really useful. It's great on grilled or steamed vegetables. In fact, steamed asparagus with Pimento Hollandaise and a shower of grated cheese tossed with grated hard-boiled eggs creates a Southern-style Asparagus Mimosa.

# PIMENTO CHEESE WAFFLES
## WITH PIMENTO SYRUP AND BACON

### SYRUP

TWO 4-OUNCE JARS SLICED PIMENTOS, WITH THEIR LIQUID

1 CUP SUGAR

1 CUP WATER

2 TABLESPOONS WHITE VINEGAR

### WAFFLES

2 LARGE EGGS

1 CUP BUTTERMILK

3 TABLESPOONS UNSALTED BUTTER, MELTED AND COOLED

1½ CUPS ALL-PURPOSE FLOUR

1 TABLESPOON BAKING POWDER

½ TEASPOON KOSHER SALT

4 OUNCES SHARP ORANGE CHEDDAR CHEESE, GRATED

ONE 2-OUNCE JAR DICED PIMENTOS, RINSED AND DRAINED

1 POUND SLICED BACON, COOKED UNTIL CRISP, FOR SERVING

Crispy, cheesy waffles with salty bacon and a swirl of sweet, peppery syrup make a super Southern breakfast treat.

◇◇◇◇◇◇◇◇◇◇◇◇◇◇◇◇◇◇◇◇◇◇◇◇◇◇◇◇◇◇◇◇◇◇◇◇◇◇◇◇◇◇◇◇◇◇◇◇◇◇◇◇◇◇◇◇

*FIRST MAKE THE SYRUP: Put the pimentos with their liquid, sugar, water, and vinegar into a high-sided medium saucepan and bring to a boil, stirring to dissolve the sugar. Remove from the heat and set aside to cool slightly. Carefully pour the mixture into a blender, vent the lid, and holding the lid down by covering it with a folded tea towel, puree the mixture until smooth.*

*Return the mixture to the saucepan, bring to a boil over medium heat, and let it bubble away, stirring occasionally, until it has reduced by half and is thick and syrupy, about 20 minutes. Cool in the pan, then transfer to a jar. The syrup will keep in the fridge for a week; just bring it to room temperature before serving.*

*MAKE THE WAFFLES: Lightly beat the eggs in a bowl, then beat in the buttermilk and butter. Add the flour, baking powder, and salt and stir until just combined. Fold in the cheese and pimentos until they are evenly distributed through the batter. Heat a waffle iron, and cook the waffles according to the manufacturers' instructions.*

*Serve the waffles warm with a few strips of bacon on top, drizzled with the pimento syrup.*

---

**RECIPE NOTE**

For Pimento Cheese Chicken and Waffles, serve some Crispy Cheddar Chicken Tenders (page 95) on top of the waffles, and douse with the syrup.

The pimento syrup is also fabulous drizzled over cream cheese or the Savory Appetizer Cheesecake (page 39).

---

# PIMENTO CHEESE POPOVERS
## WITH SCRAMBLED PIMENTO CHEESE EGGS

**POPOVERS**

2 TABLESPOONS DICED
PIMENTOS (FROM A 4-OUNCE
JAR, REMAINDER RESERVED
FOR THE EGGS)

2 LARGE EGGS

1 CUP WHOLE MILK

¾ CUP ALL-PURPOSE FLOUR

½ TEASPOON KOSHER SALT

¼ TEASPOON SWEET PAPRIKA

2 TABLESPOONS UNSALTED
BUTTER

½ CUP FINELY GRATED SHARP
CHEDDAR CHEESE

These popovers really pop with pimento cheese and are a delight filled with creamy, soft scrambled eggs jazzed up with—you guessed it—pimento cheese!

*MAKE THE POPOVERS: Drain and rinse the pimentos and pat them dry on paper towels. Set them aside to air-dry.*

*Combine the eggs, milk, flour, salt, and paprika in a blender and blend until smooth, scraping down the sides of the blender jar as needed. Let the batter rest for 1 hour.*

*Preheat the oven to 450°F. Divide the butter equally among the 6 cups of a popover pan or muffin pan. Place the pan in the oven for 3 minutes until the butter has melted and the pan is hot. Stir the cheese and pimentos into the batter with a long spoon. Do not turn the blender on again, but you can shake it around to combine the cheese and pimentos. Divide the batter equally among the cups, filling each about halfway full, and return to the oven.*

*Bake for 10 minutes. Reduce the oven temperature to 375°F, and bake for 15 minutes more, or until the popovers are puffed and golden. Do not open the oven at any time during the baking!*

*Take the pan out of the oven and, using a thin knife or skewer, loosen the popovers from the pan. Gently lift them and transfer to a wire rack. Cover with a tea towel. Serve immediately.*

## SCRAMBLED EGGS

6 LARGE EGGS

A FEW GENEROUS PINCHES OF
KOSHER SALT

A FEW PINCHES OF FRESHLY
GROUND BLACK PEPPER

¾ CUP FINELY GRATED SHARP
CHEDDAR CHEESE

RESERVED PIMENTOS
(FROM THE 4-OUNCE JAR,
SEE ABOVE; ABOUT 2
TABLESPOONS), RINSED AND
DRAINED

3 TABLESPOONS UNSALTED
BUTTER

*MAKE THE SCRAMBLED EGGS: Start the eggs about 5 minutes before the popovers come out of the oven.*

*Break the eggs into a medium bowl and whisk until well mixed; the yolks and the whites should be cohesive. Whisk in the salt, black pepper, cheese, and reserved pimentos, making sure the cheese doesn't clump together. Cut the butter into small cubes and stir them into the eggs.*

*Pour the eggs into a skillet over medium heat. When the edges start to firm up, gently push the eggs around with a spatula, letting any uncooked egg flow into the open spaces, to form soft curds. Take the pan off the heat before the eggs are completely set; the residual heat will finish them. Your eggs will be soft and creamy.*

*Slit open the top of your popovers and fill the centers with scrambled eggs. Serve immediately.*

 *PC with Bacon*

I'm from Oklahoma and I didn't grow up with pimento cheese. I only discovered it when I moved here. Now I like it with bacon. On a sandwich, I pour a little of the hot fat over it, so it gets kind of melty. Oh Lord."

—**LEEANNE**, Knoxville, Tennessee

# PIMENTO CHEESE
# GRITS CASSEROLE

1½ CUPS HEAVY CREAM

2 CUPS CHICKEN BROTH

1 TABLESPOON KOSHER SALT

A FEW GRINDS OF BLACK
PEPPER

ONE 4-OUNCE JAR DICED
PIMENTOS, RINSED AND
DRAINED

1 CUP GRITS

1 TABLESPOON GARLIC
POWDER

½ TEASPOON ONION POWDER

½ TEASPOON SWEET PAPRIKA

8 OUNCES EXTRA-SHARP
CHEDDAR CHEESE, GRATED

BUTTER, FOR GREASING THE
DISH

Grits are an iconic, beloved Southern tradition, and the best way to enjoy grits is a cheese grits casserole. That's a creamy, cheesy symphony of grits perfection, served at every holiday brunch, ladies' luncheon, or just 'cause. They are the perfect vehicle for cheese, and of course, pimentos!

*In a large heavy-bottomed pan with high sides (a 5-quart Dutch oven works great), stir together the cream and the chicken broth and a tablespoon of salt and a few grinds of black pepper to taste. Stir in the pimentos. Bring to a boil over medium heat, then, stirring constantly, pour the grits in. Continue to stir frequently until all the liquid has been absorbed and the grits have swelled. The grits will spit and sputter, so stand a little back from the pan. Taste the grits carefully as they will be hot. They should be tender with just a little bite to them; if they are still gritty or crunchy at all, add a little more cream or broth and cook until it is absorbed. Stir in the garlic powder, onion powder, and paprika. Add the grated cheese by handfuls, stirring until melted after each addition.*

*When the cheese is nicely melted, pour the grits into a well-buttered baking dish, something in the 13 x 9-inch range will do. At this point, the casserole can be refrigerated, covered, for up to a day before baking.*

*When ready to serve, preheat the oven to 350°F and bake the grits until heated through, golden, and bubbling, 35 to 40 minutes. Serve immediately.*

### RECIPE NOTES

You can use half orange extra-sharp cheddar and half white sharp cheddar if you prefer. I always use some orange cheese because it gives a beautiful cheesy color. If you'd like, hold back a half cup of grated cheese to sprinkle over the top of the casserole before baking, but watch carefully as the cheese can brown quickly.

# All Day, Every Day: Main Dishes

Serves 4

# CREAMY PIMENTO SOUP
## WITH GRILLED PIMENTO CHEESE CROUTONS

### SOUP

1 TABLESPOON OLIVE OIL

1 CUP CHOPPED ONION

2 GARLIC CLOVES

FOUR 7-OUNCE JARS DICED
PIMENTOS, RINSED AND
DRAINED

½ TEASPOON SWEET PAPRIKA

3 CUPS CHICKEN OR
VEGETABLE BROTH

1 TABLESPOON FRESHLY
SQUEEZED LEMON JUICE

½ CUP HALF-AND-HALF

KOSHER SALT

*(continued)*

Soups with floating grilled cheese croutons have become quite the trend, and here is a flavorful version with a pimento cheese twist.

*MAKE THE SOUP: Warm the olive oil in a large saucepan over medium heat. Add the onion and sauté until soft and translucent. Add the garlic and cook a minute more. Add the pimentos, sprinkle over the paprika, and cook, stirring often, for 5 minutes. Pour in the broth and bring to a boil. Cover the pan, reduce the heat to medium-low, and simmer for 20 minutes.*

*MEANWHILE, MAKE THE CROUTONS: Cut the crusts from the bread, then spread a thin layer of pimento cheese on each of 2 slices, spreading it all the way to the edge. Press the remaining slices of bread on top. Spread a thin gloss of mayonnaise on each side of the outside of both sandwiches. Sprinkle a little paprika on the mayonnaise.*

*Heat a skillet over medium heat, add the sandwiches and cook until the first side is browned and toasty and the cheese begins to melt. Flip the sandwiches and cook until toasted. Remove the sandwiches from the skillet and let rest for a few minutes, then cut each sandwich into small squares to make croutons. I find a serrated knife and a sawing motion works best to keep the cheese inside the croutons.*

*Stir the lemon juice into the soup and, using an immersion blender, if you have one, puree the soup. Or cool the soup for about 10 minutes, then puree it in batches in a regular blender until smooth. The soup can be refrigerated, covered, for up to a day before gently reheating.*

*(continued)*

## CROUTONS

4 SLICES FIRM WHITE
SANDWICH BREAD

½ CUP PREPARED PIMENTO
CHEESE

2 TABLESPOONS MAYONNAISE

SWEET PAPRIKA

*Reheat the soup over medium heat; do not boil. Stir in the half-and-half and gently heat through. Season to taste with salt. Serve the soup warm with the croutons floating on top.*

**RECIPE NOTE**

Instead of cutting them into croutons, you can serve the grilled pimento cheese sandwiches on the side; simply cut the sandwiches in half rather than into small squares. You could also spread baguette slices with pimento cheese and toast. Then float the cheesy slices on top of the soup.

# PIMENTO CHEESE SOUP
## WITH TANGY TOAST

2 TABLESPOONS OLIVE OIL

1 CARROT, FINELY DICED

1 CELERY STALK, FINELY DICED

1 MEDIUM YELLOW ONION, FINELY DICED

3 GARLIC CLOVES, MINCED

ONE 4-OUNCE JAR DICED PIMENTOS WITH THEIR LIQUID

1 TEASPOON SWEET PAPRIKA

¼ CUP ALL-PURPOSE FLOUR

4 CUPS CHICKEN BROTH

3 CUPS WHOLE MILK

1 POUND EXTRA-SHARP ORANGE CHEDDAR CHEESE, GRATED

1 TEASPOON WORCESTERSHIRE SAUCE

KOSHER SALT

FRESHLY GROUND BLACK PEPPER

HOT SAUCE (OPTIONAL)

**TANGY TOAST**

6 TO 12 SLICES FIRM WHITE SANDWICH BREAD

ABOUT 2 TABLESPOONS MAYONNAISE

SWEET PAPRIKA

KOSHER SALT

A creamy, cheesy, comforting soup with the pimento pop, and a nice little mayonnaisy nibble perched on the side.

◇◇◇◇◇◇◇◇◇◇◇◇◇◇◇◇◇◇◇◇◇◇◇◇◇◇◇◇◇◇◇◇◇◇◇◇◇◇◇◇◇◇◇◇◇◇

*MAKE THE SOUP: In a 5-quart Dutch oven, heat the olive oil over medium heat, add the diced carrot, celery, and onion, and sauté until the onion is translucent and the vegetables are soft, stirring frequently. Try to prevent browning the vegetables. When the vegetables are soft, add 1 tablespoon from the jar of pimentos and stir in. Add the garlic and stir, cooking for 1 minute more. Sprinkle the paprika over the vegetables and cook, stirring, until fragrant, about 1 minute. Add the flour, stir to coat the vegetables, and cook until there is no flour visible. Pour in the chicken broth and stir well. Increase the heat and bring the soup to a boil, then reduce the heat to medium, partially cover the pot, and simmer for 15 minutes.*

*Using an immersion blender, puree the soup until smooth. Or you can cool the soup briefly, then puree it in batches in a regular blender until smooth. Add the milk and stir well. Increase the heat to medium-high and, when the soup is just steaming, add the grated cheese in handfuls, stirring after each addition, until the cheese has melted and the soup is smooth; do not let the soup boil. Stir in the remaining pimentos and the Worcestershire sauce and season well with salt and a few grinds of black pepper to taste. If you like, add a dash or two of hot sauce.*

*Serve immediately, or set aside to cool, then refrigerate for up to 1 day. Reheat slowly over medium heat; do not let the soup boil.*

*MAKE THE TOAST: Use 1 or 2 pieces of firm white sandwich bread for each bowl of soup. Trim the crusts and spread an even not-too-thick layer of mayonnaise on each slice. Sprinkle with paprika and a little salt. Preheat the oven to 350°. Toast the bread slices in the oven on a rack set over a baking sheet, or in a toaster oven, until crispy and browned. Cut the slices into neat triangles, or into small crouton cubes.*

# PIMENTO MACARONI AND CHEESE
## WITH BACON BREAD CRUMBS

### MACARONI AND CHEESE

8 OUNCES EXTRA-SHARP
WHITE CHEDDAR CHEESE

8 OUNCES SHARP ORANGE
CHEDDAR CHEESE

4 OUNCES FONTINA CHEESE

4 OUNCES BRIE CHEESE

1 POUND TUBULAR PASTA,
SUCH AS CAVATAPPI,
MACARONI, OR SHELLS

4 CUPS (1 QUART) WHOLE
MILK

3 BAY LEAVES

3 GARLIC CLOVES

2 TABLESPOONS UNSALTED
BUTTER

2 TABLESPOONS ALL-
PURPOSE FLOUR

¼ TEASPOON FRESHLY
GRATED NUTMEG

ONE 7-OUNCE JAR DICED
PIMENTOS, RINSED AND
DRAINED

KOSHER SALT

*(continued)*

This is a macaroni and cheese for a special meal, when you really want to push the boat out with rich layered cheese nuances, the hit of tangy pimento, and a surprising, smoky, salty bacon crust.

*MAKE THE MACARONI AND CHEESE: Grate the cheddars and fontina using the disk of a food processor. Cut the rind from the Brie and cut the cheese into chunks (though if it is firm, you can grate it as well). Add to the cheddar and fontina cheeses and set aside.*

*Bring a large Dutch oven of water seasoned with 2 tablespoons of salt to a rapid boil. Add the pasta, stir, and cook according to the package instructions, for about 2 minutes less than the suggested cooking time. Drain the pasta in a large colander.*

*While the pasta is cooking, heat the milk in a saucepan with the bay leaves and smashed garlic cloves, just until bubbles form on the surface of the milk; do not boil. Remove the pan from the heat and cover with a tea towel to keep it warm and absorb the steam.*

*When the pasta is cooked and drained, return the Dutch oven to medium heat and melt the butter in it. Sprinkle the flour over the melted butter and stir until it is smooth and pale, about 3 minutes. Scoop the garlic and bay leaves from the warm milk and discard, and add the milk to the pot. Stir constantly until the sauce has thickened and is smooth, 5 to 7 minutes, scraping down the sides and bottom of the pot. Stir in the nutmeg. Dump in the cheeses and stir until everything is combined and melted and smooth. Add the pimentos and stir until evenly distributed. Add the drained pasta and stir to coat. Season to taste with salt. Scrape the pasta into a well-greased 9 x 13-inch baking dish.*

*(continued)*

### TOPPING

12 BACON SLICES

1 CUP PANKO BREAD CRUMBS

2 TABLESPOONS FRESH PARSLEY LEAVES

½ TEASPOON SWEET PAPRIKA

2 TABLESPOONS UNSALTED BUTTER

MAKE THE TOPPING: *Preheat the oven to 400°F. Place the bacon slices on a wire rack set over a rimmed baking sheet and bake in the oven until crispy, 20 to 25 minutes. Remove from the oven, pat the bacon dry with paper towels, and set aside to cool.*

*Clean any stray bits of cheese from the food processor bowl and fit with the metal blade. Crumble in the bacon, add the panko, parsley, and paprika and process until you have very fine crumbs and the bacon is broken down. Melt the butter in a small bowl in the microwave, add to the crumbs, and process until they are damp. Spread the bacon bread crumbs evenly over the top of the macaroni and cheese and lightly pat them down. The casserole can be refrigerated, covered, for several hours before baking.*

*When ready to bake, preheat the oven to 350°F. Cover the baking dish with aluminum foil and bake for 20 minutes. Remove the foil and bake for 10 minutes more, or until heated through and bubbling and the bread crumbs are toasted.*

### ➡ A Quick Dinner

In the process of testing recipes for this book, I have always had pimento cheese ingredients on hand, so I've taken to whipping up this quick pasta bowl for nights when I want a quick, easily prepared dinner. I cook about 4 ounces of pasta, usually a short shape like shells or penne. Technically that should be two servings, but I admit to eating the whole lot myself.

While the pasta is cooking, I put about 3 ounces of cheddar cheese cut into small pieces into the bowl of my mini food processor, add some undrained pimento—a 2-ounce jar or a tablespoon or so from an open, larger jar—and 2 big spoonfuls of mayo. If I have anything else around, or I am in the mood, I might toss in a garlic clove, a small bit of onion, a dash of Worcestershire sauce or hot sauce. Then I blend it all up until it is as smooth as it will go.

When the pasta is ready, I dip out about 1/3 cup of the cooking water and drain the pasta. With the machine running, I pour the cooking water into the processor and process until everything is smooth, then transfer it to the empty pasta pot. I let it boil until it is thickened and reduced, add the drained pasta, stir to coat, and continue cooking until the sauce just coats the pasta. If I have the energy, I sprinkle on some grated cheddar.

# WEEKNIGHT
# PIMENTO MACARONI AND CHEESE

8 OUNCES MACARONI OR
CAVATAPPI PASTA

2 TABLESPOONS UNSALTED
BUTTER, PLUS MORE FOR
GREASING THE DISH

8 OUNCES SHARP ORANGE
CHEDDAR CHEESE

8 OUNCES SHARP WHITE
CHEDDAR CHEESE

4 OUNCES FONTINA CHEESE

ONE 4-OUNCE JAR DICED
PIMENTOS, RINSED AND
DRAINED

2 CUPS WHOLE MILK

¼ CUP ALL-PURPOSE FLOUR

½ TEASPOON GARLIC POWDER

½ TEASPOON SWEET PAPRIKA

½ TEASPOON DRY MUSTARD
POWDER

¼ TEASPOON ONION POWDER

DASH OF FRESHLY GRATED
NUTMEG

KOSHER SALT

FRESHLY GROUND BLACK
PEPPER

This is my go-to recipe for quick, homemade mac and cheese, perfect for a weeknight family dinner. It may be quick and easy, but it is incredibly creamy and pops with the flavor of pimento cheese.

◇◇◇◇◇◇◇◇◇◇◇◇◇◇◇◇◇◇◇◇◇◇◇◇◇◇◇◇◇◇◇◇◇◇◇◇◇◇◇◇◇◇◇◇◇◇◇◇◇◇◇◇

*Cook the pasta according to package instructions in a large pot of rapidly boiling well-salted water. Drain and return to the pot off the heat.*

*Stir in the butter to melt and toss to coat the pasta and prevent the pasta from sticking together. Set aside to cool.*

*Preheat the oven to 375°F. Thoroughly butter a 2-quart baking dish.*

*Grate all the cheeses and toss with the cooled pasta, reserving a few handfuls for the top. Stir in the pimentos.*

*Whisk together the milk, flour, spices, and salt and black pepper to taste in a bowl. Whisk well for at least a minute until the flour is completely mixed with the milk. Pour the mixture over the pasta and cheese and stir thoroughly until well combined. Spoon the mixture into the buttered dish and spread out to create an even surface. Sprinkle the remaining cheese on top.*

*Bake for about 30 minutes, or until golden on top and bubbling and heated through.*

*You've heard the story of the Southern cook and the Northern reporter, right?*

COOK: We make a great pimento cheese.

REPORTER: What kind of cheese?

COOK: Pimento cheese.

REPORTER: What cheese?

COOK: Pimento cheese. You have had pimento cheese before, right?

REPORTER: I've never even heard of it.

COOK: Bless your heart.

—EATLOCALMEMPHIS.ORG

# SIMPLE PIMENTO CHEESE
## BREAD AND BUTTER PUDDING

8 SLICES FIRM WHITE
SANDWICH BREAD

1 CUP PIMENTO CHEESE
SPREAD

BUTTER, FOR GREASING THE
BAKING DISH

3 LARGE EGGS

1 CUP WHOLE MILK

2 TEASPOONS DIJON
MUSTARD

KOSHER SALT

FRESHLY GROUND BLACK
PEPPER

### RECIPE NOTES

This is a very simple dish
that relies heavily on
the flavor of the pimento
cheese you use, so let
that be your guide. You
could add more mustard,
some hot sauce, chopped
parsley, chopped scallions,
or Worcestershire sauce
to the egg mixture.

This is a savory take on a classic English sweet, in which bread and butter are sandwiched together and cooked in a sweet custard. Use your favorite version of pimento cheese and flavor the egg and milk mixture to taste.

Cut the crusts from the bread, and then spread 4 slices with a layer of pimento cheese, making sure you spread it all the way to the edges of the bread. Top with the remaining slices of bread to make sandwiches. Cut the sandwiches into quarters, so you have 16 little sandwiches.

Butter a 2-quart square or rectangular baking dish. Place the little sandwiches in the dish in two rows, with the first sandwich pointy end up, and the second pointy end down and so on. Tuck any remaining sandwiches in to fill any large gaps.

Whisk the eggs, milk, and mustard together until completely blended. Season to taste with salt and black pepper, but be aware of how salty your pimento cheese is and don't go overboard. Pour the egg mixture over the sandwiches, making sure to moisten all the exposed bread. Cover the dish with plastic wrap and gently press down. You don't have to smush the top, just submerge the sandwiches slightly in the custard.

Refrigerate the pudding for at least an hour, but up to 6 hours is just fine.

When ready to bake, preheat the oven to 350°F. Cover the baking dish with aluminum foil and bake for 30 minutes. Remove the foil and bake for 15 minutes more, or until the custard has set and the top is golden brown.

## Pimento Cheese Night

When I launched into my previous career in party planning, I always counseled my clients and brides to build a menu that was personal to them. To serve a favorite cookie from Aunt Susie's recipe, or pasta to commemorate your first date at the Italian restaurant, or pralines to pay homage to a Louisiana family heritage. It became sort of signature of the events I planned. I built multi-tiered Krispy Kreme groom's cakes, served late-night Krystal (to you Northerners—Southern White Castle) hamburgers on silver salvers, and filled champagne buckets with ice cream sandwiches. So I always asked: what is a personal favorite food you'd love to serve at your event? I cannot tell you the number of times pimento cheese was on the list. So, with the help of a favorite caterer, elegant little pimento cheese sandwiches became a regular feature and frequent request.

I planned a party in Mississippi about an hour or so outside of Memphis that was a fun, country affair by the river. We fried catfish and hush puppies and made little barbecue sandwiches and, of course, served the pimento cheese delights as a passed hors d'oeuvre. At the end of the night, my caterer friend sent me home with a tray of sandwiches, bless her. As I drove home through the dark Delta night, well past one o'clock in the morning, I snacked on a few of those little sandwiches. When I got home, sore and exhausted, I left everything in the car except that tray. I took it inside to wrap up the remaining sandwiches to last me through another week of crazy parties. They were gone. I'd eaten every one. This was a roasting pan—like 10 x 8 x 3-inches deep—gone in one sitting. It may have been the best night of my life.

Serves 6

# CREAMY PIMENTO CHEESE AND
# CHICKEN PASTA

4 BONELESS, SKINLESS
CHICKEN BREAST HALVES

12 OUNCES SPAGHETTI,
BROKEN IN HALF

5 TABLESPOONS UNSALTED
BUTTER

1 YELLOW ONION, FINELY
DICED

2 GARLIC CLOVES, MINCED

½ TEASPOON SWEET PAPRIKA

3 TABLESPOONS ALL-
PURPOSE FLOUR

3 CUPS CHICKEN BROTH

1 (8-OUNCE) BLOCK OF CREAM
CHEESE, CUBED AND AT ROOM
TEMPERATURE

2 CUPS FINELY GRATED
CHEDDAR CHEESE

1 (4-OUNCE) JAR DICED
PIMENTOS, RINSED AND
DRAINED

Simple, comforting, and creamy, this pimento cheese version of a comfort food classic will please even the pickiest eaters.

Preheat the oven to 350°. Place the chicken breasts in a baking dish and season well with salt and pepper. Cover the dish with foil and bake the chicken until it is cooked through, to an internal temperature of 165°, about 25 minutes.

Cook the pasta in a large pot of well-salted water, cooking it slightly underdone, about 1 minute less than the package instructions say. Drain the pasta in a large colander and rinse it with cool water. Melt 1 tablespoon of the butter in the pot and toss the pasta in it to coat. This prevents the noodles from sticking together. Return the pasta to the colander.

Rinse and dry the pasta pot and return it to the stove. Melt the remaining 4 tablespoons butter, then add the onions and cook over medium-high heat until soft and translucent, about 8 minutes. Add the garlic and paprika and cook one minute more. Sprinkle over the flour and stir until the onions are coated and thick. Whisk in the chicken broth and cook, stirring, until thickened, about 10 minutes. Whisk in the cream cheese, a bit at a time, whisking well after each addition. It may look a bit separated or curdled at the beginning; just keep whisking and it will smooth out. When all the cream cheese is smooth, stir in 1¼ cups of the grated cheese and whisk until smooth. Stir in the pimentos and season well with salt and pepper.

*Cut and shred the chicken breasts into small bite-size pieces. You want it to incorporate well with the spaghetti. Stir the pasta and the chicken into the sauce in the pan, stirring to coat completely and distribute everything evenly. Tongs are helpful in this task. Taste and add more salt if needed. Spread the mixture into a well-buttered 9 x 13-inch baking dish, smoothing the top to an even layer. Sprinkle the remaining 3/4 cup of cheddar cheese over the top. The casserole can be cooled, covered, and refrigerated eight hours at this point.*

*When ready to cook, preheat the oven to 350° and bake the casserole, covered with foil, for 30 minutes or until it is hot throughout and bubbling. Remove the foil and bake a further 5 minutes to melt the cheese on top. Serve immediately.*

# CHEDDAR CHEESE GNUDI
## WITH PIMENTO ROMESCO SAUCE

### GNUDI

4 OUNCES EXTRA-SHARP AGED CHEDDAR CHEESE

ONE 15-OUNCE CONTAINER WHOLE-MILK RICOTTA

1 LARGE EGG YOLK

1 CUP ALL-PURPOSE FLOUR, PLUS MORE FOR DUSTING

1 TEASPOON SALT, PLUS MORE FOR BOILING THE GNUDI

1/4 TEASPOON SWEET PAPRIKA

### ROMESCO SAUCE

1 SLICE WHITE SANDWICH BREAD

3/4 CUP SLIVERED ALMONDS

3 GARLIC CLOVES, CHOPPED

ONE 14.5-OUNCE CAN DICED TOMATOES

ONE 7-OUNCE JAR (OR TWO 4-OUNCE) JARS DICED PIMENTOS, WITH THEIR LIQUID

1/2 TEASPOON SWEET PAPRIKA

1/2 TEASPOON SALT

1/4 TEASPOON SMOKED PAPRIKA (PIMENTÓN)

4 TABLESPOONS OLIVE OIL

This recipe shows a totally different side of our pimento cheese flavors; the southern Mediterranean meets the American South—pillowy soft ricotta dumplings with a hint of tangy cheddar and a nutty, peppery sauce from Spain. Use a very sharp, flavorful cheddar cheese.

*MAKE THE GNUDI: Grate the cheese on the fine holes of a box grater. Measure out ¾ cup into a large bowl; reserve the remaining cheese to sprinkle on the finished dish. Add the ricotta and the egg yolk to the cheese in the bowl and stir with a spatula until combined. Add the flour, salt, and paprika and stir with the spatula, then knead with your clean hands just until the flour is incorporated and you have a stiff dough.*

*Line a baking sheet with waxed paper. Lightly flour a work surface and place the dough on it. Pat the dough out to a square and cut it into 4 even pieces. I like to use a bench scraper, but a long, sharp knife works as well. Roll out each piece into an even rope about 12 inches long. Cut each rope into little pillows, about ½ inch long. They need to be as close to the same size as possible, so cut one then use it as a guide when cutting the rest. Transfer the cut gnudi to the lined baking tray. At this point, you can cover the tray with a clean, dry tea towel and place it in the refrigerator for up to an hour before cooking the gnudi.*

*MAKE THE ROMESCO SAUCE: Toast the bread until it is lightly golden and crisp. Toast the almonds in a dry skillet on the stovetop over medium-high heat until they are golden and fragrant. Tear the bread into pieces and put into the bowl of a food processor. Add the almonds and the sliced garlic. Process until you have fine crumbs.*

*Pour in the tomatoes and pimentos with their liquid. Add the sweet paprika, salt, and smoked paprika. Turn the processor on and drizzle in the olive oil until you have a smooth sauce. Process for about 5 minutes. Scoop the romesco sauce into a bowl and set aside.*

*(continued)*

COOK THE GNUDI: *Bring a large Dutch oven or pot of water with a table-spoon of salt to a rolling boil. Pour the romesco sauce into a large, deep skillet and heat over medium-low. When the water is boiling, add the gnudi, a few at a time, then give them all a gentle stir. Working carefully, using a ladle or a handled measuring cup, dip out ½ cup of the boiling pasta water and add it to the romesco sauce to loosen it up. Stir well and increase the heat until the sauce is bubbling.*

*The gnudi need about 3 minutes to cook. When they are floating at the top of the water, cook them for 30 seconds more, then, using a slotted spoon, lift them out of the water and transfer to the skillet of sauce. Gently stir them around to coat them with the sauce and cook until warmed through. Scoop the gnudi and sauce into bowls and sprinkle with the remaining grated cheddar cheese. Serve immediately.*

**RECIPE NOTE**

For a variation, the gnudi can also be pan-fried in a little butter, then served with some Pimento Cheese Compound Butter (see page 106) melted on top

# CRISPY CHEDDAR CHICKEN TENDERS
## WITH PIMENTO DIP

**CHICKEN**

3 CHICKEN BREASTS

1 CUP BUTTERMILK

4 OUNCES MEDIUM CHEDDAR CHEESE

2 CUPS PANKO BREAD CRUMBS

½ TEASPOON SWEET PAPRIKA

½ TEASPOON FRESHLY GROUND BLACK PEPPER

½ TEASPOON KOSHER SALT

**DIP**

1 CUP SOUR CREAM

½ CUP MAYONNAISE

ONE 2-OUNCE JAR DICED PIMENTOS, RINSED AND DRAINED

½ TEASPOON KOSHER SALT

½ TEASPOON SWEET PAPRIKA

FRESHLY GROUND BLACK PEPPER

A "pimento-cheesified" version of the family-friendly classic. The chicken is crispy with cheese and the dip is smooth and creamy with just the right hit of pimento.

*PREPARE THE CHICKEN: Cut the chicken breasts lengthwise into thin tenders. Put them into a zip-top bag with the buttermilk and swish them around to coat each tender. Seal the bag and place in the refrigerator to marinate for at least 1 hour, but several hours is fine.*

*MEANWHILE, MAKE THE DIP: Place the sour cream, mayonnaise, pimentos, salt, paprika, and black pepper in the bowl of a food processor or a blender. Blend until completely smooth. Scrape into a bowl, cover, and refrigerate for several hours to allow the flavors to meld.*

*CONTINUE MAKING THE CHICKEN TENDERS: Grate the cheese on the fine holes of a box grater to produce 1 cup. In a small bowl, mix together the panko, paprika, black pepper, and salt with a fork, then add the cheese. Using the fork and your clean fingers, mix the cheese and bread crumbs together. The cheese tends to clump up, so toss it all around until the cheese and crumbs are evenly distributed.*

*Place a wire rack over a rimmed baking sheet, spray it with cooking spray, and set on your workspace. Remove the chicken from the fridge and pull out one tender. Shake it off to remove excess liquid, then drop it in the crumbs and roll it around, pressing the crumbs in to fully coat it. Place the tender on the rack and repeat the process with the remaining chicken and crumb coating. Place the baking sheet in the fridge for at least 30 minutes before baking, but several hours is fine. This will help the coating adhere to the chicken during baking.*

*Preheat the oven to 400°F. Bake the chicken tenders until they are crispy on the outside and cooked through, about 20 minutes. Serve immediately with the dip.*

# PIMENTO CHEESE
# CHICKEN POT PIE

### FOR THE CRUST

1¾ CUP ALL-PURPOSE FLOUR

¼ CUP YELLOW CORNMEAL

¾ CUP (1½ STICKS) COLD BUTTER

½ CUP GRATED SHARP CHEDDAR CHEESE

1 (2-OUNCE) JAR DICED PIMENTOS, RINSED, DRAINED, AND PATTED DRY

1 TEASPOON SALT

½ CUP VERY COLD WATER

Creamy pot pies are a perfect homey comfort food. But the concept has been tainted by years of bad, processed, prepackaged and even fast-food versions, as well as recipes that call for condensed soups and canned chicken. None of that sounds the least bit appealing to me. Now when you mention pot pie, many people get that glazed-over look, imagining the foil pan of gloopy, doughy, microwaveable mess. For some people I know, pot pie is no longer a dish they make with pride, but a guilty secret from a box they only eat when no one can see them. What a shame.

Ah, but freshly made pot pie, with quality ingredients and a homemade crust is worth the effort. My pimento cheese version adds bacon, pimentos, and sharp cheddar to the mix—even the crust is pimento cheese!

◇◇◇◇◇◇◇◇◇◇◇◇◇◇◇◇◇◇◇◇◇◇◇◇◇◇◇◇◇◇◇◇◇◇◇◇◇◇◇◇◇◇◇◇◇◇◇◇◇

*FOR THE CRUST: Place the flour, cornmeal, butter, cheese, pimentos, and salt in the bowl of a food processor. Turn the machine on, and drizzle in the cold water until the dough comes together in a ball that pulls away from the sides of the bowl. Turn the dough out onto a large piece of plastic wrap and flatten it out into a disk. Wrap tightly and place in the refrigerator for at least half an hour, but longer is fine.*

*FOR THE FILLING: Preheat the oven to 350°. Place the chicken breasts in a baking dish and cover it tightly with foil. Cook until the chicken breasts are cooked through (165° internal temperature), about 25 minutes. Uncover and set aside to cool. When cool, cut the chicken into bite-sized pieces.*

*Dice the bacon into small pieces (I find scissors a great tool for this) and sauté in a large skillet until crispy. Remove the bacon to a paper towel–lined plate with a slotted spoon. Let the bacon grease cool a little, then carefully pour it into a measuring cup and set it aside. Let the skillet cool until it is safe to touch, then wipe out any burned bits or dark brown spots. Return the skillet to medium-high heat and pour in 2 tablespoons bacon grease. Sauté the*

## FOR THE FILLING

3 BONELESS SKINLESS
CHICKEN BREASTS

10 SLICES OF BACON

1 YELLOW ONION, FINELY
DICED

2 CELERY STICKS, FINELY
DICED

1 CARROT, FINELY DICED

2 CLOVES GARLIC, FINELY
MINCED

3 TEASPOONS CHOPPED
FRESH THYME

½ CUP WHITE WINE

1 (4-OUNCE) JAR DICED
PIMENTOS, RINSED AND
DRAINED

3 TABLESPOONS BUTTER

3 TABLESPOONS FLOUR

1½ CUPS CHICKEN BROTH,
AT ROOM TEMPERATURE

1½ CUPS MILK, AT ROOM
TEMPERATURE

2 CUPS GRATED SHARP
CHEDDAR CHEESE

1 TABLESPOON CHOPPED
PARSLEY

SALT AND PEPPER TO TASTE

onion, celery, and carrot until they just begin to soften. Cover the skillet and cook until the vegetables are soft, and the onions and celery are translucent, stirring occasionally. Add the garlic and thyme and cook a few more minutes until fragrant. Pour in the white wine and cook, stirring, until all the liquid has evaporated. Stir in the pimentos, then add the butter and stir until melted. Sprinkle the flour over the vegetables and stir until the flour is blended in. Slowly pour in the chicken broth and milk, stirring constantly, until the sauce thickens. Stir in the grated cheese until it is melted and smooth. Stir in the parsley, the bacon pieces, and the cubed chicken and season well with salt and pepper. Set aside to cool.

TO ASSEMBLE: Spoon the cooled chicken filling into a 4-quart baking dish. Remove the crust dough from the fridge and roll it out on a lightly floured surface until it is big enough to fit over the top of the filling. Carefully drape the crust directly over the filling and tuck it down around the sides. Cut a couple of slashes in the top to let steam escape. At this point, the pie can be covered and refrigerated for several hours.

When ready to cook, preheat the oven to 350°. Bake the pot pie until the crust is golden and the filling is cooked through and bubbling, about 40–45 minutes.

Serve immediately.

# CHICKEN ENCHILADAS
## WITH PIMENTO CHEESE SAUCE

### CHICKEN FILLING

1 TEASPOON KOSHER SALT, PLUS MORE AS NEEDED

1 TEASPOON MILD CHILI POWDER

½ TEASPOON GROUND CUMIN

¼ TEASPOON SWEET PAPRIKA

DASH OF CAYENNE PEPPER

A FEW GRINDS OF BLACK PEPPER

4 BONELESS, SKINLESS CHICKEN BREAST HALVES

2 TABLESPOONS OLIVE OIL

1 ONION, DICED

ONE 4-OUNCE JAR SLICED PIMENTOS, RINSED AND DRAINED

1 GARLIC CLOVE, FINELY MINCED

½ CUPS CHICKEN BROTH

½ CUP HEAVY CREAM

12 CORN TORTILLAS

*(continued)*

Pimento Cheese really does have a million uses. The creamy, cheesy flavors create an interesting twist on classic chicken enchiladas with just a hint of Southwestern flavors.

◇◇◇◇◇◇◇◇◇◇◇◇◇◇◇◇◇◇◇◇◇◇◇◇◇◇◇◇◇◇◇◇◇◇◇◇◇◇◇◇◇◇◇◇◇◇◇◇◇

*Preheat the oven to 350°F. Spray a small baking dish with nonstick cooking spray.*

*PREPARE THE FILLING: In a small bowl, mix together the salt, chili powder, cumin, paprika, cayenne, and black pepper. Place the chicken breasts in the baking dish and sprinkle both sides generously with the seasoning mix.*

*Bake the chicken in the oven until it reaches an internal temperature of 165°F, 20 to 25 minutes. Remove from the oven and transfer the chicken breasts to a plate to cool.*

*When the chicken is cool enough to handle, shred the meat into small strands using your hands or two forks. Drizzle the oil in a skillet large enough to hold the chicken meat. Add the onion and sauté until it is soft and translucent, about 8 minutes. Add the sliced pimentos and the garlic and cook for 2 minutes more. Add the chicken broth and the heavy cream and cook over medium-high heat, stirring frequently, until the liquid has reduced to a creamy sauce that will lightly coat the meat, 10 to 12 minutes. Remember, this is to fill tortillas, so if the sauce is too wet it will leak out. Add the shredded chicken and stir to coat evenly with the sauce.*

*ASSEMBLE THE ENCHILADAS: When the creamy filling is cool enough to handle, grease a 9 x 13-inch baking dish with nonstick cooking spray. Wrap the tortillas in damp paper towels and microwave for 30 to 45 seconds to soften them. Fill a tortilla with chicken filling, sprinkle over a little cheddar cheese (using about ½ cup total for all the tortillas), roll it up and place the*

*(continued)*

## PIMENTO CHEESE SAUCE

2 TABLESPOONS UNSALTED
BUTTER

2 TABLESPOONS ALL-
PURPOSE FLOUR

1½ CUPS CHICKEN BROTH

ONE 2-OUNCE JAR DICED
PIMENTOS, RINSED AND
DRAINED

1 CUP (8 OUNCES) SOUR
CREAM

2 CUPS GRATED SHARP
CHEDDAR CHEESE

KOSHER SALT, AS NEEDED

tortillas, seam side down, in the prepared baking dish. I find it easiest to place just enough filling in each tortilla so it will roll into a compact package, then go back and stuff more filling in the ends when they are snugly in the baking dish. Repeat with all the remaining tortillas, chicken, and cheese. You can rewrap the tortillas in damp towels and microwave again if they begin to get stiff. Set the enchiladas aside.

MAKE THE PIMENTO CHEESE SAUCE: Melt the butter in a saucepan over medium heat. Whisk in the flour and cook until smooth. Pour in the chicken broth and whisk until smooth. Cook the sauce for 5 minutes, or until it has thickened and is smooth and creamy.

Stir in the diced pimentos, then stir in the sour cream and cook until it is heated through. Add 1½ cups of the grated cheese, a handful at a time, and whisk to melt each addition before adding the next. Taste and add salt if needed.

Pour the pimento cheese sauce over the enchiladas, spreading it out into an even layer. Make sure you completely cover the tortillas. You can sprinkle some of the remaining cheese over the top if you'd like. At this point, you can cool the enchiladas, cover with aluminum foil, and refrigerate for several hours.

When ready to bake, preheat the oven to 350°F. Bake the enchiladas, uncovered, for 30 minutes, or until the sauce is bubbling and everything is heated through. Serve immediately.

# PIMENTO
# CHEESESTEAK SANDWICHES

1 POUND TOP ROUND STEAK

1 MEDIUM YELLOW ONION

¼ CUP OLIVE OIL

¼ CUP WORCESTERSHIRE SAUCE

4 OUNCES SHARP CHEDDAR CHEESE

1½ OUNCES CREAM CHEESE

¼ TEASPOON GRANULATED SUGAR

¼ TEASPOON SWEET PAPRIKA

¼ TEASPOON GARLIC POWDER

¼ TEASPOON ONION POWDER

½ TEASPOON KOSHER SALT, PLUS MORE AS NEEDED

½ CUP WATER, PLUS MORE AS NEEDED

ONE 4-OUNCE JAR SLICED PIMENTOS, WITH THEIR LIQUID

SALT

FRESHLY GROUND BLACK PEPPER

½ CUP WHOLE MILK

4 SOFT HOAGIE ROLLS, TOASTED

I'm no expert on Philly Cheesesteaks, so this may be more the idea in my head than any actual authentic version, but this is a darn good sandwich, in no small part due to the creamy cheese sauce created by Casey Barber of the Web site goodfoodstories.com.

◇◇◇◇◇◇◇◇◇◇◇◇◇◇◇◇◇◇◇◇◇◇◇◇◇◇◇◇◇◇◇◇◇◇◇◇◇◇◇◇◇◇◇◇◇◇◇◇◇◇◇◇◇

*Put the steak in the freezer for about 20 minutes to firm it up; this makes it easier to slice thinly. Slice the onion in half, then slice into thin half-moons. Put the sliced onion in a zip-top bag. When the steak is firm, use your sharpest knife to slice it into the thinnest slices you can manage. Place the steak slices in a separate zip-top bag. (Don't be tempted to do this in the same bag; the onions and steak cook separately, and it is a pain to separate them out!)*

*Blend together the olive oil and Worcestershire sauce in a glass measuring cup and divide it evenly between the bags of onions and the steak. Toss both bags to coat the contents with the marinade, then set in the refrigerator to marinate for at least an hour, but several hours is even better.*

*When you are ready to assemble the sandwiches, grate the cheddar cheese and put it into the bowl of a mini food processor along with the cream cheese, sugar, paprika, garlic and onion powders, and salt and let come to room temperature.*

*Pour the onions and their marinade into a large skillet and sauté over medium-high heat until they are soft and pliable. Add the water, cover the skillet, and cook until the onions are slightly caramelized and soft, stirring occasionally, about 15 minutes. Add a dash more water, as needed, to prevent the onions from sticking or burning. Add the pimentos with their liquid and stir well. Cover the skillet and cook about 5 minutes more.*

*(continued)*

*Drop in the beef and its marinade and stir well until the beef begins to brown. Cover the skillet and cook for 5 minutes. Remove the lid and cook, stirring, until the beef is cooked through and any liquid has reduced to a light glaze. Season to taste with salt and black pepper. Cover the skillet to keep the filling warm.*

*Heat the milk in a small saucepan until it is very hot; do not boil. You can also heat it in the microwave in a measuring jug for about 45 seconds, just until bubbles form. Turn on the food processor with the cheese mixture in it and pour in the milk through the feed tube. Process until the sauce is smooth, scraping down the sides of the bowl as necessary.*

*Spoon the meat filling into the toasted hoagie rolls and top with the cheese sauce.*

 *Everyone's Got an Opinion*

At a recent Southern Foodways Alliance Symposium, Chef Ashley Christensen of Poole's Diner in Raleigh, North Carolina, prepared a marvelous twelve-course vegetarian feast that started with beautiful appetizer boards featuring Mason jars of pimento cheese. I was seated with an old friend from Memphis who relocated to New Orleans. We were discussing the recipe he uses for pimento cheese in his restaurant—it's basically his sister-in-law's—and how that compares to our favorite Memphis versions. When the chef began her talk about the inspiration for the meal, she said how much she loves it when her food gets a reaction, and that she just knew people were eating her pimento cheese, but talking about their own recipe. My friend and I couldn't help but laugh. And I'll admit, a jar of the pimento cheese left the party in my purse.

# PIMENTO CHEESE
## STUFFED BURGERS

### FOR THE PIMENTO CHEESE FILLING

8 OUNCES SHARP ORANGE
CHEDDAR CHEESE

4 OUNCES CREAM CHEESE

½ TEASPOON
WORCESTERSHIRE SAUCE

¼ TEASPOON SWEET PAPRIKA

¼ TEASPOON GARLIC

¼ TEASPOON ONION POWDER

¼ TEASPOON KOSHER SALT

1 (2-OUNCE) JAR DICED
PIMENTOS, RINSED AND
DRAINED

### FOR THE BURGERS

2 POUNDS GROUND CHUCK

2 TABLESPOONS
WORCESTERSHIRE SAUCE

2 TABLESPOONS KETCHUP

2 TABLESPOONS DIJON
MUSTARD

1 TEASPOON BLACK PEPPER

1 TEASPOON KOSHER SALT

8 HAMBURGER BUNS

The first question you are going to ask is "Can't I just use the pimento cheese that's already in my fridge?" And yes, you can. But my mission has been to perfect the use of pimento cheese, and this smooth, creamy version produces the yummy, gooey center you want from these burgers.

◇◇◇◇◇◇◇◇◇◇◇◇◇◇◇◇◇◇◇◇◇◇◇◇◇◇◇◇◇◇◇◇◇◇◇◇◇◇◇◇◇◇◇◇◇◇◇◇◇◇

FOR THE PIMENTO CHEESE: Grate the cheese on the grating blade of a food processor. Switch to the metal blade, add the cream cheese, Worcestershire, paprika, garlic, onion, and salt and process until smooth and combined. Add the pimentos and process until you have a smooth paste.

Line a plate with waxed paper and scoop the pimento cheese into balls and place on the plate. I use a large 2 tablespoon cookie scoop. Wet your fingers, then press each ball into a little patty. Place in the refrigerator for at least 30 minutes, but several hours is fine. You want the pimento cheese patties to be firm for easier stuffing.

FOR THE BURGERS: Take the beef out of the fridge to take the chill off. Working with fridge-chilled meat is not pleasant. Add the other ingredients and use your clean hands to blend it all together. Make sure everything is mixed in, but do not knead it around too much. Divide the mixture into 8 equal portions. Take one portion, flatten it out in your hands and place a pimento cheese patty in the center. Bring the meat up around the cheese and pinch it all together to seal in the cheese. I've never really discovered an art to this; just work the meat around the pimento cheese until you can't see it at all.

Refrigerate the burgers on a plate lined with waxed paper for about 30 minutes.

*When ready to cook, preheat the oven to 450° F. Line a rimmed baking sheet with foil and place a wire rack in it. Spray the rack with cooking spray, then place the burgers about 1 inch apart on the rack. Bake in the oven until the burgers are cooked through, about 10–12 minutes. Poke the meaty part of the burger with a pointy knife. If the juices run clear, you're good to go. Watch carefully—the longer you cook, the more likely the cheese is to run out. Let the burgers rest for 5 minutes out of the oven before serving on buttered and toasted buns.*

*You can grill these burgers, too. Heat the grill to medium high and grill each patty about 5 minutes on the first side. Flip, cover the grill, and grill until cooked through, about 5 more minutes.*

**RECIPE NOTE**

You can half this recipe, or freeze any extra uncooked patties individually wrapped in plastic for another night.

# PAPRIKA PEPPER STEAK
## WITH PIMENTO CHEESE COMPOUND BUTTER

**COMPOUND BUTTER**

2 TABLESPOONS DICED PIMENTOS

8 TABLESPOONS (1 STICK) UNSALTED BUTTER, SOFTENED

½ CUP FINELY GRATED EXTRA-SHARP ORANGE CHEDDAR CHEESE

1 GARLIC CLOVE

½ TEASPOON KOSHER SALT

**STEAK**

2 TEASPOONS SWEET PAPRIKA

1½ TEASPOONS CRACKED BLACK PEPPER

1½ TEASPOONS KOSHER SALT

FOUR 4- TO 6-OUNCE FILET STEAKS

Coarse, cracked pepper really adds to the crust on these steaks. I keep a jar of cracked black pepper in my pantry, but if you don't, use the coarsest grind on your pepper mill.

MAKE THE COMPOUND BUTTER: Rinse and drain the pimentos well. Place the pimentos on a double layer of paper towels and pat them as dry as you can get them. Scrape them onto a cutting board and, using a sharp knife, chop them as finely as you can. When they are chopped, pat them dry with a paper towel again.

Put the butter in a bowl and break it up with a fork. Add the pimentos and the grated cheddar. Put the garlic through a press, or mash it on the cutting board, then add it and the salt to the butter. Mash everything together with the fork until it is well blended and the ingredients are evenly distributed. Scrape the butter onto a piece of plastic wrap and shape it into an even log. Wrap it tightly in plastic wrap, twisting the ends closed, and refrigerate for several hours. The compound butter will keep in the fridge for 1 week, or store in the freezer for up to 3 months.

COOK THE STEAK: Preheat the oven to 350°F.

Mix together the paprika, cracked black pepper, and salt. Pat the steaks dry with paper towels and let come to room temperature. Spread the paprika mix on a plate and press the steaks into the spices, creating a nice crust on both sides of each steak. Press the spices firmly into the meat.

(continued)

**RECIPE NOTE**

There will be more compound butter than you need for the steaks. You can serve extra if you like, or freeze the remainder for your next steak night. This compound butter is also good on chicken or fish.

*Preheat a cast-iron skillet over high heat until it is very hot; a drop of water when sprinkled on it should sizzle and bounce. You might want to turn on your extractor fan now! Place the steaks into the hot skillet and cook until the spice mix is seared into the meat and forms a nice crust. Do not turn the steaks until they lift easily from the skillet. Using tongs, gently turn the steaks and cook the opposite sides. Transfer the skillet to the oven and cook the steaks to your desired degree of doneness.*

*When the steaks go in the oven, slice 8 rounds of compound butter about ⅛-inch thick and set aside. When the steaks are cooked, remove the skillet from the oven, place 2 slices of butter on top of each steak, cover the skillet with aluminum foil, and let the steaks rest for a few minutes before serving to allow the juices to redistribute.*

# BEEFY PIMENTO CHEESE
# NOODLE BAKE

8 OUNCES CURLY EGG
NOODLES

1 POUND GROUND BEEF

1 SMALL YELLOW ONION,
FINELY CHOPPED

2 CARROTS, FINELY DICED OR
GRATED

ONE 4-OUNCE JAR DICED
PIMENTOS WITH THEIR LIQUID

2 GARLIC CLOVES, MINCED

1 TABLESPOON CHOPPED
FRESH OREGANO

1 CUP (8 OUNCES) TOMATO
SAUCE

KOSHER SALT

FRESHLY GROUND BLACK
PEPPER

1 CUP WHOLE MILK

2 TABLESPOONS ALL-
PURPOSE FLOUR

½ TEASPOON SWEET PAPRIKA

¼ TEASPOON FRESHLY
GRATED NUTMEG

8 OUNCES SHARP CHEDDAR
CHEESE, GRATED

While working on this project, I took to thinking of this dish as "pimento cheeseroni." It's a nice weeknight version of a classic comfort casserole, with the tang of pimentos and a creamy, but not overwhelming, cheese sauce.

Cook the noodles in well-salted water in a large Dutch oven according to the package directions, but cook about 2 minutes less than the suggested cooking time, as a slightly firmer noodle will stand up better to baking. Drain the noodles and toss with a drizzle of olive oil to prevent sticking.

Crumble the ground beef into the Dutch oven and cook over medium-high heat until it starts to brown, breaking it up with a sturdy spatula. Add the onion, carrots, and pimentos and cook until the beef is no longer pink and the onions are soft and translucent. Add the garlic and oregano and cook for 2 minutes more; do not let the garlic brown. Add the tomato sauce and cook for about 5 minutes more, or until the liquid has slightly reduced. Stir the noodles into the beef mixture. Season well with salt and black pepper and scoop the meat and noodle mixture into a greased 7 x 11-inch baking dish.

Pour the milk into a medium saucepan and whisk in the flour, paprika, and nutmeg until well blended. Cook, whisking constantly, until the sauce has thickened, about 3 minutes. Reserve 1 cup of the cheese, then whisk the rest into the sauce and cook until the sauce is smooth and the cheese has melted. Scrape the cheese sauce over the top of the noodle mixture in the baking dish and spread it out into an even layer. Sprinkle the reserved 1 cup of cheese over the top. At this point, you can cool, cover, and refrigerate the casserole for several hours.

When ready to bake, preheat the oven to 350°F and remove the dish from the fridge while the oven is preheating. Bake the casserole until cooked through and bubbling and the cheese has melted, about 20 minutes. Let sit for about 5 minutes before serving.

Serves 4

# PIMENTO
# SHRIMP AND CHEDDAR GRITS

## GRITS

2 CUPS CHICKEN BROTH,
PLUS MORE AS NEEDED

2 CUPS HEAVY CREAM

4 TABLESPOONS (½ STICK)
UNSALTED BUTTER

1 CUP STONE-GROUND GRITS

2½ TEASPOONS KOSHER SALT

SEVERAL GRINDS OF BLACK
PEPPER

8 OUNCES SHARP CHEDDAR
CHEESE, GRATED

## SHRIMP

1 TEASPOON SWEET PAPRIKA

½ TEASPOON DRY MUSTARD
POWDER

¼ TEASPOON SMOKED
PAPRIKA (PIMENTÓN)

¼ TEASPOON KOSHER SALT

A FEW GRINDS OF BLACK
PEPPER

*(continued)*

The classic "Shrimp and Grits" originated in the South Carolina low country, but the concept has spread throughout the South, with as many variations as there are cooks who make it.

◇◇◇◇◇◇◇◇◇◇◇◇◇◇◇◇◇◇◇◇◇◇◇◇◇◇◇◇◇◇◇◇◇◇◇◇◇◇◇◇◇◇◇◇◇

*COOK THE GRITS: In a deep-sided large pan (grits tend to spatter) over medium-high heat, stir together the broth, cream, and butter until the butter has melted and all the ingredients have come to a low boil. Stir in the grits, salt, and black pepper and reduce the heat to low. Cover and cook for 30 to 45 minutes, stirring frequently to prevent scorching. The grits should be tender and the liquid absorbed. You may add a bit more broth if needed. Stir in the grated cheese, a handful at a time, until it has melted and is smooth before adding the next handful.*

*When cooked, the grits can be kept, covered, for an hour or so, then slowly reheated over low heat, stirring in a little extra broth as needed.*

*COOK THE SHRIMP: Mix together the paprika, mustard, smoked paprika, salt, black pepper, and cayenne. Pat the shrimp dry with paper towels and place on a plate. Sprinkle the spice mix liberally over both sides of the shrimp, turning them over to make sure they get a good coating. Place the plate of shrimp in the fridge for 30 minutes to 1 hour.*

*When the shrimp are ready, sauté the bacon pieces in a wide skillet over medium-high until crispy. Using a slotted spoon, transfer the bacon to a plate lined with paper towels. Carefully pour the bacon grease into a small bowl. Spoon 2 tablespoons of grease back into the skillet and heat over medium-high. Add the shrimp and sear briefly—just a few seconds per side—to seal in the spice mixture; you do not want to cook the shrimp through. Transfer the shrimp to a clean plate, or you can scoot the bacon to one side and use the same plate.*

*(continued)*

DASH OF CAYENNE PEPPER

1 POUND LARGE SHRIMP, PEELED AND DEVEINED (I PREFER FRESH GULF SHRIMP OR FROZEN WILD AMERICAN SHRIMP)

6 BACON SLICES, CUT INTO SMALL PIECES

ONE 4-OUNCE JAR SLICED PIMENTOS, WITH THEIR LIQUID

¾ CUP CHOPPED SCALLIONS, WHITE, LIGHT GREEN, AND A LITTLE DARK GREEN (FROM A BIG BUNCH)

ONE 14.5-OUNCE CAN DICED TOMATOES

ABOUT 1 CUP CHICKEN BROTH

2 TABLESPOONS ALL-PURPOSE FLOUR

A QUARTER OF A LARGE LEMON

FINELY CHOPPED FRESH PARSLEY, FOR GARNISH

Reduce the heat to medium and add more bacon grease to the skillet so that you have about 4 tablespoons, then drop in the pimentos and the scallions. Sauté until the pimentos and scallions are soft. As they release some liquid, you can scrape the tasty brown bits from the bottom of the pan.

While the vegetables are cooking, drain most of the juice from the tomatoes into a measuring cup. You can just hold the top of the can askew and drain out what you can—no need to dirty a strainer. Add enough chicken broth to the tomato liquid to make 1 cup and set aside.

When the vegetables are soft, add the tomatoes to the skillet and cook until the tomatoes are heated through and start to soften, breaking up any large pieces. Sprinkle the flour over the vegetables and stir to coat. There should not be any white flour visible. Pour in the tomato liquid and broth mixture and stir, scraping the bottom of the pan. Reduce the heat a little and let the liquid bubble away until it is nice and thick, stirring to avoid scorching. Squeeze over the juice from the lemon quarter, making sure you've removed seeds, and stir in. Add the shrimp to the skillet, cover, and cook for 5 to 8 minutes until the shrimp are cooked through. You can add a bit more broth if you would like a saucier version.

Spoon the grits into four shallow bowls and spoon over the shrimp and sauce. Sprinkle over the crispy bacon pieces and chopped parsley. Serve immediately.

# A Little Something on the Side: Vegetables & Sides

# PIMENTO CHEESE
# TOMATO PIE

## PIE PASTRY

1¼ CUPS ALL-PURPOSE FLOUR

½ TEASPOON KOSHER SALT

½ TEASPOON SUGAR

8 TABLESPOONS (1 STICK) UNSALTED COLD BUTTER, CUT INTO SMALL PIECES

2 TO 4 TABLESPOONS ICE WATER

## TOMATO PIE

3 LARGE TOMATOES

KOSHER SALT

FRESHLY GROUND BLACK PEPPER

PASTRY FOR ONE 9-INCH PIE CRUST (SEE ABOVE)

8 SCALLIONS, WHITE AND PALEST GREEN PARTS ONLY, FINELY SLICED

2 TABLESPOONS CHOPPED FRESH PARSLEY

*(continued)*

Tomato Pie is another true Southern summer classic. One of the favorite ways many Southerners enjoy fresh tomatoes is lightly salted and sandwiched between white bread spread with a slick of mayonnaise. This pie seems to be an outgrowth of that simple pleasure: fresh tomatoes layered with mayonnaise and cheese in a pie crust.

*MAKE THE PIE PASTRY: Put the flour, salt, and sugar into the bowl of a food processor fitted with the metal blade and pulse a few times to combine. Drop in the small pieces of cold butter and pulse several times until the mixture is crumbly, but some minute pieces of butter are still visible. Sprinkle the ice water over, a tablespoon at a time, and pulse to combine. When the pastry dough just comes together, dump it out onto a lightly floured surface and pat it into a disk about ¾ inch thick. Wrap the disk in plastic wrap and refrigerate for at least 1 hour before rolling.*

*PREPARE THE TOMATOES: Cut the ends off the tomatoes and discard, then slice them about ½ inch thick. Lay the tomato slices on a double layer of paper towels and sprinkle generously with salt. Let the tomatoes sit for at least an hour, turning them over after 30 minutes and salting the opposite sides. Sprinkle the second side with black pepper as well.*

*When ready to bake the crust, preheat the oven to 350°F. Remove the pastry from the refrigerator and place the pastry disk on a lightly floured work surface. Using a floured rolling pin, roll out the pastry to a round about 14 inches in diameter, large enough to fit a 9-inch pie plate. Carefully drape the pastry over the rolling pin and transfer to the pie dish. Gently press the dough into the bottom and sides of the pie dish. Cover the pastry shell with parchment paper and fill with dried beans or ceramic pie weights. Bake for 15 minutes, then remove from the oven, remove the paper and weights, and set the pie crust aside to cool.*

*(continued)*

ONE 4-OUNCE JAR DICED
PIMENTOS, RINSED AND
DRAINED

1½ CUPS GRATED EXTRA-
SHARP CHEDDAR CHEESE

¾ CUP MAYONNAISE

½ TEASPOON SWEET PAPRIKA

1 GARLIC CLOVE

ASSEMBLE THE PIE: *When the crust has completely cooled, layer half the tomato slices over the bottom. Sprinkle the scallions, parsley, and half of the pimentos over the tomatoes, then ½ cup of the grated cheddar cheese. Layer the remaining tomatoes on top.*

*Mix together the mayonnaise, the remaining 1 cup cheddar cheese, remaining pimentos, and paprika in a small bowl. Put the garlic through a press or very finely mince it with a sharp knife and stir it into the mayonnaise. Spread the mixture over the tomatoes, spreading it all the way to the edges.*

*Bake the pie at 350°F for 30 minutes, or until golden brown around the edges and the top. Let the pie cool for 10 minutes before slicing and serving.*

# PIMENTO CHEESE
# PARTY POTATOES

ONE 2-POUND PACKAGE
FROZEN SOUTHERN-STYLE
HASH-BROWN POTATOES
(SMALL, CUBED POTATOES,
NO ONIONS OR SEASONINGS)

8 OUNCES SHARP CHEDDAR
CHEESE, GRATED

ONE 4-OUNCE JAR DICED
PIMENTOS, RINSED AND
DRAINED

4 TABLESPOONS (½ STICK)
UNSALTED BUTTER, PLUS
MORE FOR BUTTERING THE
BAKING DISH

3 TABLESPOONS ALL-
PURPOSE FLOUR

3 CUPS WHOLE MILK

1½ TEASPOONS KOSHER SALT

½ TEASPOON ONION POWDER

½ TEASPOON PAPRIKA

½ TEASPOON FRESHLY
GRATED NUTMEG

DASH OF CAYENNE PEPPER

I call these party potatoes because they make easy work of a big side dish for a party meal. I have made these countless times for Christmas and New Year's Eve parties, making three or four batches to feed the crowds. The frozen diced potatoes are the trick, saving the work of peeling and cubing pounds of potatoes. Add some cooked, crumbled bacon or diced ham and you'd have a nice breakfast casserole.

◇◇◇◇◇◇◇◇◇◇◇◇◇◇◇◇◇◇◇◇◇◇◇◇◇◇◇◇◇◇◇◇◇◇◇◇◇◇◇◇◇◇◇◇◇◇

*Butter a 9 x 13-inch baking dish. Shake the potatoes into a colander and set aside to thaw for about 15 minutes, just to make sure there are no ice crystals clinging to the potatoes. There is no need to thaw them completely.*

*Break up the potatoes and toss with the cheese and pimentos in the baking dish, doing your best to evenly distribute everything.*

*Melt the butter in a medium saucepan, then whisk in the flour. Cook until smooth and pale in color, then slowly stir in the milk. Stir constantly until the sauce has thickened, then stir in the salt, onion powder, paprika, nutmeg, and cayenne. Cook, stirring constantly, until the mixture comes to a boil. Pour the sauce over the potatoes in the baking dish, spreading it out to cover the surface.*

*At this point, the casserole can be cooled and refrigerated, covered, for up to a day before baking.*

*When ready to bake, preheat the oven to 350°F. Uncover the dish and bake for 50 to 60 minutes until the mixture is set and the top is lightly golden.*

Serves 4; makes 2 cups sauce

# FRIED GREEN TOMATOES
## WITH PIMENTO CHEESE SAUCE

### PIMENTO CHEESE SAUCE

¾ CUP MAYONNAISE

½ CUP BUTTERMILK

6 OUNCES SHARP CHEDDAR
CHEESE, GRATED

ONE 2-OUNCE JAR DICED
PIMENTOS, RINSED AND
DRAINED

1 TEASPOON
WORCESTERSHIRE SAUCE

½ TEASPOON SWEET PAPRIKA

### TOMATOES

3 LARGE GREEN TOMATOES

1 LARGE EGG

½ CUP BUTTERMILK

½ CUP STONE-GROUND
CORNMEAL

¼ CUP ALL-PURPOSE FLOUR

½ TEASPOON SWEET PAPRIKA

½ TEASPOON KOSHER
SALT, PLUS MORE FOR THE
TOMATOES

½ TEASPOON FRESHLY
GROUND BLACK PEPPER

DASH OF CAYENNE PEPPER

VEGETABLE OIL, FOR FRYING

There is perhaps no food that has come to be associated in the wider world with Southern cuisine more than fried green tomatoes. Fried green tomatoes are delicious with a scoop of your favorite pimento cheese melted over the top, but this creamy sauce brings the flavor of pimento cheese to the party without overwhelming the beauty of the tomatoes. Spread some sauce on bread, add a couple of fried green tomatoes and some crispy bacon, and you've got one hell of a sandwich.

MAKE THE SAUCE: Place all the ingredients for the sauce in a blender and blend until smooth. Store, covered, in the refrigerator for up to 5 days.

PREPARE THE TOMATOES: Place a wire rack over a rimmed baking sheet and set by your stovetop. Preheat the oven to 200°F.

Slice the tomatoes about ⅓ inch thick. Lay the tomato slices on a double layer of paper towels and sprinkle with salt. Set aside to drain while you prepare the coating.

Beat the egg and the buttermilk together in a shallow bowl. On a deep plate or baking sheet, combine the cornmeal, flour, paprika, salt, black pepper, and cayenne.

Dip the tomato slices in the buttermilk mixture, then in the cornmeal, pressing the coating onto each side. Shake off any excess coating and place the tomatoes on the wire rack set over the baking sheet while the oil is heating.

(continued)

**RECIPE NOTE**

For a special salad variation, you can spoon the Pimento Cheese Sauce over a wedge of iceberg lettuce. Sprinkle some grated cheddar and rinsed and drained pimentos over the wedge, and add some chopped crispy bacon.

When all the tomatoes are coated, heat about ½ inch of vegetable oil in a wide, deep skillet over medium heat to 375°F. Fry the tomatoes, a few at a time, until crispy and golden, 3 to 5 minutes per side. Don't crowd the pan. Return the fried tomatoes to the wire rack over the baking sheet to drain. When all the tomatoes have been fried, you can place them in the oven to keep warm for about 15 minutes.

Serve the tomatoes hot with the Pimento Cheese Sauce drizzled over the top, or on the side as a dip.

### It All Changed

My mother would sometimes make homemade pimento cheese with what my grandfather called "rat cheese," the bright orange cheddar coated in red wax. Homemade was more special, but she nearly always had a plastic container of Ruth's Salads Pimento Cheese in the refrigerator drawer. Only in the South would grated cheese and mayonnaise be considered a salad. I remember the familiar red and black logo with its loopy, cursive font and the plastic lid that snapped tight against the bright orange spread.

As a small child, I considered pimento cheese a decidedly grown-up flavor and didn't care for it in the least—it must have been those piquant pimentos! At some point, around middle school, it all changed. I'm not certain if it was a change in my palate or I was trying to be a grown-up and wanted to emulate my mother, but I grew to love pimento cheese. She'd lather it on slices of white bread or serve it cradled in the curve of a celery stick. It makes my mouth water just thinking about it.

—**VIRGINIA WILLIS**, chef and food writer

Serves 6 to 8

# PIMENTO CHEESE
# SQUASH CASSEROLE

2 POUNDS YELLOW SUMMER
CROOKNECK SQUASH

¾ CUP LIGHTLY SALTED
WATER

1 SWEET YELLOW ONION,
PREFERABLY VIDALIA

2 TABLESPOONS UNSALTED
BUTTER

2 TABLESPOONS OLIVE OIL

3 LARGE EGGS

1 CUP (8-OUNCES) SOUR
CREAM

ONE 4-OUNCE JAR DICED
PIMENTOS, RINSED AND
DRAINED

KOSHER SALT

FRESHLY GROUND BLACK
PEPPER

8 OUNCES MILD CHEDDAR
CHEESE, GRATED

45 BUTTERY ROUND
CRACKERS, SUCH AS TOWN
HOUSE, TO MAKE 2 CUPS
CRUMBS

2 TABLESPOONS CHOPPED
FRESH PARSLEY

½ TEASPOON SWEET PAPRIKA

2 TABLESPOONS UNSALTED
BUTTER, MELTED

Summer squash casserole falls into that vaunted category of "any real South-ern cook has her own recipe . . ." And this squash casserole is mine, paired with the magic of pimento cheese.

Wash and dry the squash and slice it into rounds about ¼ inch thick. You can use a mandoline, or the slicing disk on a food processor (then you can switch disks to grate the cheese). Place the squash slices in a large sauté pan and add the lightly salted water. Cook the squash, covered, over medium-high heat un-til the squash is just tender, about 5 minutes. Drain the squash in the colander, shaking gently several times to remove as much water as possible.

Dice the onion. Wipe out the sauté pan, add the butter with olive oil and melt over medium heat. Add the onion and cook slowly until soft and translucent, stirring frequently. You want the onion to be translucent and soft, but not browned. Add the onion to the drained squash in the colander and stir gently to combine. Set aside to cool.

Preheat the oven to 375°F. Spray a 2-quart baking dish with nonstick cooking spray.

Beat the eggs in a large bowl, add the sour cream and pimentos, and stir until smooth. Season with salt and a liberal amount of black pepper. Shake any accumulated liquid from the squash and onion and add to the bowl. Add ½ cup of the grated cheese and stir to gently coat the squash with the sour cream mixture. Taste and add more salt if needed. Scrape the squash into the pre-pared baking dish and smooth the top. Sprinkle the remaining cheese evenly over the squash.

(continued)

*Place the crackers in a zip-top bag and crush very finely using a rolling pin or the heel of your hand. Mix the cracker crumbs, chopped parsley, paprika, and melted butter in the bag and shake to combine. Sprinkle the crumb topping over the squash and spread it out to evenly cover.*

*Cover the dish loosely with aluminum foil and bake for 30 minutes, or until golden brown, puffed, and bubbling at the edges. Remove the foil for the last 10 minutes of baking to brown the crumb topping. Serve immediately.*

*The casserole can be refrigerated, covered, for up to a day before baking.*

### Pawleys Island

I will always remember my introduction years ago to pimento cheese at Pawleys Island, South Carolina: pimento cheese, Wonder Bread, salty air, crashing waves, and vacation forever linked in my mind. This Northerner, originally from Nebraska, now living in Cincinnati, was smitten.

—SHARON, Cincinnati, Ohio

Serves 4

# PIMENTO CHEESE
# GREEN BEANS

1 POUND FRESH GREEN
BEANS, TRIMMED

2 TABLESPOONS UNSALTED
BUTTER, PLUS MORE FOR
BUTTERING THE BAKING DISH

1 CUP DICED ONION (ABOUT
1 SMALL ONION)

ONE 4-OUNCE JAR SLICED
PIMENTOS, RINSED AND
DRAINED

2 GARLIC CLOVES, FINELY
MINCED

¼ CUP MAYONNAISE

¼ CUP HEAVY CREAM

4 OUNCES SHARP CHEDDAR
CHEESE, GRATED

KOSHER SALT

FRESHLY GROUND BLACK
PEPPER

"Green Bean Casserole." The very mention can strike fear into the hearts of man. I cannot abide the standard version with canned green beans and canned soup and fried bits of something, but a casserole made with fresh green beans and a creamy, tangy sauce is a whole different affair. Add some pimentos and a little cheddar cheese and you are now speaking my language.

Cut the trimmed green beans into roughly 1-inch pieces. Bring a large skillet of water to a boil and drop in the beans. Boil for about a minute, just until the bright color of the beans comes out. Drain the beans and plunge into ice water to cool. Drain again.

Wipe out the skillet and melt the butter over medium-high heat. Add the diced onion and cook, stirring frequently, until the onion is soft and just beginning to turn a pale caramel brown, about 8 minutes. Add the drained pimentos, stir, and cook for about 2 minutes. Stir in the garlic and cook for a minute more; do not let the garlic brown. Remove the skillet from the heat and stir in the green beans until everything is evenly distributed. Set aside to cool.

Preheat the oven to 350°F. Butter a 8 x 8-inch baking dish.

Mix together the mayonnaise and cream in a small bowl, then add it to the green beans, stirring to coat the beans completely. Stir in the cheese until evenly distributed. Season with salt and pepper to taste.

Spread the beans into the prepared baking dish. Cover the dish with aluminum foil and bake for 20 minutes. Remove the foil and bake for 10 minutes more. Serve immediately.

The casserole can be refrigerated, covered, for several hours before baking.

# PIMENTO CHEESE
# CREAMED SPINACH

3 (12-OUNCE) PACKAGES
FROZEN CHOPPED SPINACH,
THAWED

4 TABLESPOONS UNSALTED
BUTTER

½ MEDIUM YELLOW ONION,
FINELY CHOPPED

3 GARLIC CLOVES, FINELY
MINCED

4 OUNCES CREAM CHEESE

1 CUP WHOLE MILK

1 CUP (8-OUNCES) SOUR
CREAM

¼ CUP MAYONNAISE

1 TABLESPOON DIJON
MUSTARD

1 LARGE EGG, LIGHTLY
BEATEN

2 CUPS SHARP CHEDDAR
CHEESE, GRATED

1 (4-OUNCE) JAR DICED
PIMENTOS, RINSED AND
DRAINED

KOSHER SALT AND PEPPER
TO TASTE

½ CUP DRY BREAD CRUMBS

Creamed Spinach is a family favorite that I couldn't help but tinker with to make a pimento cheese version.

Wrap the spinach in a clean tea towel and squeeze out as much moisture as possible.

Melt 2 tablespoons butter in a large Dutch oven and add the diced onions. Cook over medium heat until soft and translucent, stirring frequently, about 5 minutes. Add the garlic and cook one minute more. Remove the pot from the heat and stir in the spinach, breaking it up as you go. Cut the cream cheese into small pieces and stir it into the spinach. Add the milk, sour cream, mayonnaise, and mustard and stir to combine until completely incorporated. Making sure the spinach mixture is cool, stir in the egg. Add 1½ cups of grated cheese and the pimentos and stir to distribute all the ingredients evenly. Taste, and add salt and pepper as needed.

Scrape the spinach into a 2-quart baking dish, smoothing the top to an even surface.

Mix the remaining ½ cup grated cheese and panko in a small bowl. Melt the remaining 2 tablespoons butter and add it to the bread crumbs and stir to thoroughly combine. Sprinkle the bread crumbs evenly over the top of the spinach.

The casserole can be cooled, covered, and refrigerated for up to a day at this point. When ready to bake, preheat the oven to 350°. Bake until golden and set, about 40 minutes. Serve immediately.

## An Intensely Personal Pursuit

I have a mayonnaise aversion, but when I moved south from New York and had my first taste of proper pimento cheese bound with just enough handmade mayonnaise, everything changed. The trick, I learned, is the right mayonnaise along with the proper blend of really sharp white cheddar and a milder orange cheese. And heat. You need to kiss it with enough cayenne so the heat announces itself but just barely. You let it sit at room temperature so the flavors meld, then chill it overnight. When you're ready to eat, spread it into celery that has been chilling in an ice-water bath. Of course, people will argue with this approach. This is what is so great about pimento cheese. It is an intensely personal pursuit.

—KIM SEVERSON, *New York Times* national food correspondent

# GREEN PEA
## PIMENTO CHEESE SALAD

1 POUND FROZEN GREEN
PEAS

8 OUNCES SHARP CHEDDAR
CHEESE

½ CUP MAYONNAISE

½ CUP SOUR CREAM

1 TEASPOON
WORCESTERSHIRE SAUCE

½ TEASPOON SWEET PAPRIKA

½ TEASPOON FRESHLY
GROUND BLACK PEPPER

¼ TEASPOON KOSHER SALT

DASH OF CAYENNE PEPPER

DASH OF HOT SAUCE

1 CUP FINELY DICED ONION

ONE 4-OUNCE JAR DICED
PIMENTOS, RINSED AND
DRAINED

I found myself reading a version of this recipe over and over again, in a host of community cookbooks. Many of those recipes used odd things from bottles and some pretty strange extras, and every one of them used peas from a can, many insisting on a very specific silver can. This is my updated version using frozen peas and a jazzed-up dressing. I will admit, I was a little dubious at first, but this is a really delicious and unique salad that elicited surprised delight from multiple generations.

*Tumble the peas into a colander and thaw completely. Dice the cheddar cheese into small cubes. I like them about the same size as the peas, but this does take a little time, so be patient.*

*When the peas are thawed, in a large bowl whisk together the mayonnaise, sour cream, Worcestershire sauce, paprika, black pepper, salt, cayenne, and hot sauce. Add the diced onion and drained pimentos and stir to combine. Gently fold in the cheese cubes and the peas until thoroughly coated with the dressing. Cover the bowl and refrigerate for at least 2 hours to let all the flavors meld. The salad can be kept, covered, in the refrigerator for up to 2 days.*

# PIMENTO CHEESE
# CORN PUDDING

BUTTER, FOR GREASING THE
BAKING DISH

2 LARGE EGGS

ONE 16-OUNCE CAN CREAMED
CORN

ONE 16-OUNCE CAN WHOLE
KERNEL CORN, DRAINED

8 TABLESPOONS (1 STICK)
UNSALTED BUTTER, MELTED

1 CUP (8-OUNCES) SOUR
CREAM

½ TEASPOON SWEET PAPRIKA

1 TEASPOON KOSHER SALT

½ TEASPOON FRESHLY
GROUND BLACK PEPPER

DASH OF CAYENNE PEPPER

ONE 8½-OUNCE PACKAGE
CORN MUFFIN MIX (I PREFER
JIFFY BRAND)

1½ CUPS GRATED EXTRA-
SHARP CHEDDAR CHEESE

ONE 4-OUNCE JAR DICED
PIMENTOS, RINSED AND
DRAINED

Corn pudding is one of my all-time favorite comfort food dishes. I always make it for Thanksgiving—though we don't need one more thing on the table—just so I can make extra and hide it away in the back of the overstuffed fridge to have as my own personal leftovers. I have made every recipe for corn pudding I have ever seen, ones that involved shucking and scraping dozens of ears of corn and ones that use a bag of frozen kernels. And believe me, the recipe below is the best one of all of them. It probably started its life on the back of a box, and I probably picked it out of some community cookbook. Whatever the case, I am very sentimental about it. I have added the joy that is pimento cheese flavoring, but the basic recipe creates a light, fluffy, creamy dish— everything a perfect corn pudding should be.

Preheat the oven to 350°F. Grease a 9 x 13-inch baking dish.

Beat the eggs in a large mixing bowl, then add both cans of corn, the melted butter, and sour cream and mix thoroughly. Stir in the paprika, salt, black pepper, and cayenne. Fold in the corn muffin mix, cheese, and pimentos and mix to incorporate all the ingredients.

Scrape the mixture into the prepared baking dish and smooth the top. Bake for 30 to 35 minutes until puffed and golden and firm in the center.

Serve immediately.

# A Great Way to Eat Corn on the Cob

One of my favorite ways to eat corn on the cob is Mexican *elotes*: corn spread with a thin layer of mayonnaise, dusted with chili powder, and sprinkled with Cotija cheese. So I took the idea to pimento cheese town. Spread your corn with a thin layer of mayo, dust lightly with paprika (smoked paprika is particularly good here), and then roll those cobs in some very finely grated sharp cheddar cheese.

# PIMENTO CHEESE
# RISOTTO

4 CUPS CHICKEN BROTH

1 TABLESPOON UNSALTED
BUTTER

1 TABLESPOON OLIVE OIL

5 SCALLIONS, WHITE AND
LIGHT GREEN PARTS ONLY,
FINELY DICED

1 GARLIC CLOVE, FINELY
MINCED

1½ CUPS ARBORIO OR
SIMILAR RISOTTO RICE

1 TEASPOON SWEET PAPRIKA

½ CUP WHITE WINE

ONE 4-OUNCE JAR DICED
PIMENTOS, RINSED AND
DRAINED

5 OUNCES SHARP CHEDDAR
CHEESE, DICED

KOSHER SALT

SWEET PAPRIKA

GRATED CHEDDAR CHEESE, TO
GARNISH

CHOPPED SCALLION TOPS, TO
GARNISH

Since I learned to make risotto, and realized it was something you could actually make—not a mysterious only-in-a-restaurant dish—it has become one of my favorite comfort foods. So it seems only natural that I pair it with my Southern comfort favorite, pimento cheese.

Bring the chicken broth to a simmer in a saucepan over medium heat.

Melt the butter with the olive oil in a large sauté pan over medium-high heat and add the scallions. Cook until the scallions are soft and translucent, about 5 minutes. Add the garlic and cook for another minute, then stir in the rice and paprika. Cook, stirring constantly, until the rice is translucent around the edges of the grains, just a few minutes. Add the wine and cook, stirring, until it has been absorbed.

Add the warm chicken broth, about ½ cup at a time, stirring frequently. Let each addition of stock completely absorb before adding the next. This will take about 18 minutes. When all the broth has been added and absorbed, stir in the pimentos, then add the cheese cubes a handful at a time, stirring until each handful has melted in before adding the next.

Season the risotto to taste with salt, and serve immediately, sprinkled with some paprika, a little grated cheese, and some chopped scallion tops if you like.

### RECIPE NOTE

Pimento Cheese-ancini: Refrigerate any leftover risotto overnight and when it is firm, scoop out about 2 tablespoons at a time and form it into a ball. Stuff a small cube of cheddar cheese in the center, and enclose completely with the risotto. Roll the balls in beaten egg, then in bread crumbs, and fry in about 4 inches of vegetable oil until brown and crispy. Delicious when served hot with Pimento Cheese Sauce for dipping.

## ❋ About the Author ❋

Perre Coleman Magness is the cook behind the Web site The Runaway Spoon, therunawayspoon.com, which focuses on creative recipes with a definite Southern slant. Her work also appears in *Edible Memphis, OKRA: The Magazine of the Southern Food and Beverage Museum,* and *The Christian Science Monitor* Online.

Perre has studied food and cooking around the world, mostly by eating, but also through serious study. Coursework at Le Cordon Bleu London and intensive courses in Morocco and Thailand as well as seminars in Mexico, Santa Fe, and Memphis have broadened her culinary skill and palate. But her kitchen of choice is at home, cooking like most people, experimenting with unique but practical ideas.

College in Connecticut and graduate school in England taught her to cherish her Southern roots, to learn and explore all the flavors that make the South so special. Perre has traveled extensively, from Egypt to Zimbabwe, India to South Africa, Peru to Indonesia, Burma to Spain, Tunisia to Cambodia, and just keeps going. She can relate at least two meals from each destination as her primary memories of each journey.

## ✳ Sources ✳

BRITISHCHEESE.COM
*The Cambridge World History of Food,* edited by Kenneth F. Kipple and Kriemhild Conne Ornelas.

*"Creating a (New) Southern Icon: The Curious History of Pimento Cheese,"* robertfmoss.com, 2011.

DUKESMAYO.COM
*"It Was There for Work: Pimento Cheese in the Carolina Piedmont,"* by Emily Wallace, 2010.

# INDEX

# INDEX